Classic Country Inns of America

The Pacific Coast and The Southwest

CLASSIC COUNTRY INNS OF AMERICA
VOLUME 3

Inns of
The Pacific Coast
and
The Southwest

BY PETER ANDREWS
PHOTOGRAPHED BY
LILO RAYMOND, GEORGE W. GARDNER
AND STEVE NORTHUP

AN ARCHITECTURAL DIGEST BOOK

THE
KNAPP PRESS
LOS ANGELES

HOLT,
RINEHART
AND WINSTON
NEW YORK

Library of Congress Cataloging in Publication Data

Andrews, Peter, 1931–
  Inns of the Pacific coast and Southwest.

  (His Classic country inns of America; v. 3)
  1. Hotels, taverns, etc.—Pacific States.
2. Hotels, taverns, etc.—Southwestern States.
I. Raymond, Lilo, Gardner, George W. and
'Northup, Steve, joint authors.   II. Title.
III. Series.
TX909.A583   647'.9479   77-
71352
ISBN 0-03-042846-7

First Edition

10 9 8 7 6 5 4 3 2 1

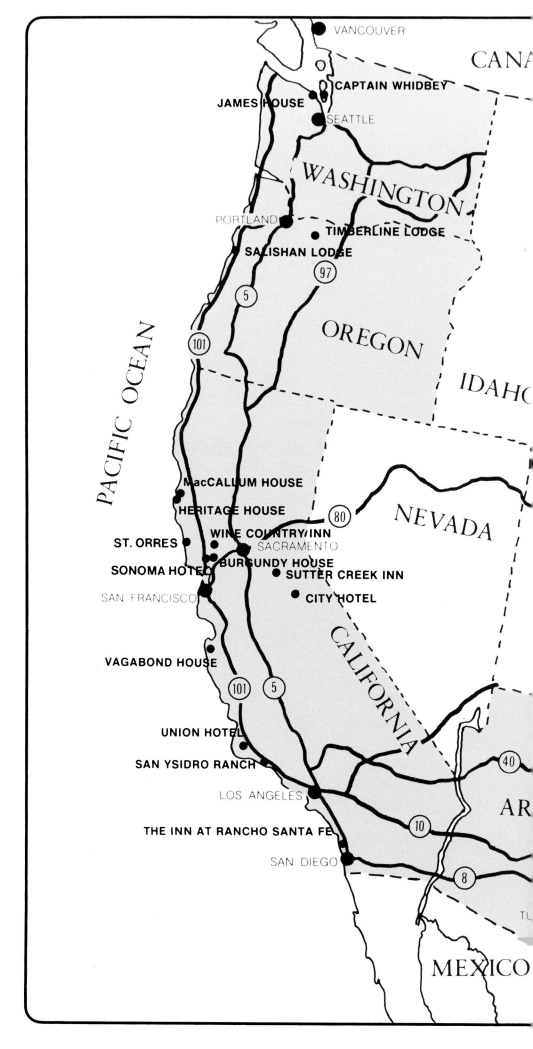

CONTENTS

* Photographed by George Gardner
† Photographed by Lilo Raymond
‡ Photographed by Steve Northup

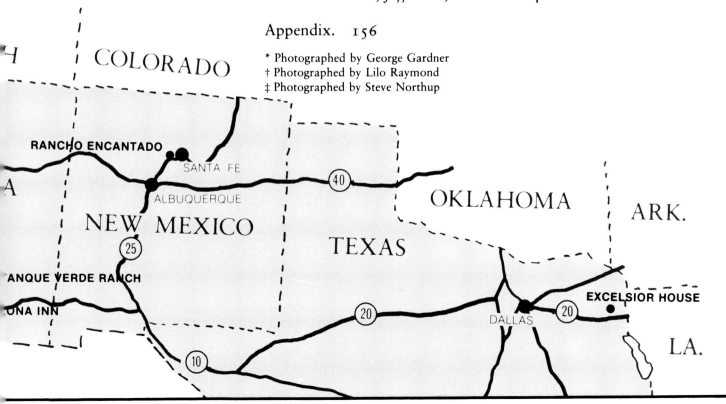

Bill Norris
and daughter Allison
MacCallum House

REFUGE AND REFRESHMENT

Innkeeping in the Far West is part of a tradition that is older than the
nation. In 1769, the Franciscan monks who came to California from
Spain began to forge a chain of missions along the Pacific coast from
what is now San Diego up to Sonoma. The journey north took some
twenty-one days, and it was essential that, at the end of each day,
travelers be certain of food and shelter. Later, in the wake of men like
Jedediah Smith, trappers and mountain men found way stations and
trading posts that would take them in. No part of America has a richer
heritage of hospitality than the West where, two hundred years ago,
a safe refuge could mean the difference between life and death.

Few western inns today can trace their architectural history back for
more than one hundred years, but visitors sometimes come across a
trace of an earlier refuge. Part of the adobe built by Franciscans in
1826 still stands at San Ysidro Ranch in Montecito. Many western inns
of a more recent vintage were established during the incredible period
of growth and expansion that marked the California Gold Rush. Others
were put up at the turn of the century, and a few were built within the
last ten years.

Innkeeping is a quixotic calling; people are drawn to it for any
number of reasons. There is the natural satisfaction that comes from
extending hospitality to the traveler, but there is also an additional
imperative—the challenge of creating a unique and ideal environment.

Eric Black and Richard Wasserman had been building houses for
friends in Marin County when they purchased an old fishing lodge on
the coast near Gualala early in the 1970s. The urge to design in wood
was strong, and with the help of friends, scavanged materials and a
gritty commitment equal to the isolation of the spot, they found
themselves innkeepers, four years later, of St. Orres, a domed Russian
fantasy structure that could have been the setting for a Pushkin novel.

7

Dick and Teri Langdon
Union Hotel

Jane Way
Sutter Creek Inn

When Lowell Bogart, a geologist from Oklahoma, and his wife, Barbara, made an overnight decision to buy the James House in Port Townsend, Washington, they were grateful that the former innkeepers stayed on for a while to put them through their paces. "They broke us in proper," Lowell recalls. "They'd walk into the front parlor and pretend to be visitors and ask all kinds of things. 'How's the clamming?' 'When's high tide?' 'How strong does the wind blow?' It was a real education."

Two of the inns shown here were started as acts of compassion during a troubled time. Timberline Lodge, on Mount Hood in Oregon, is the product of a huge depression-era federal project to develop

Jim Lavenson
San Ysidro Ranch

9

Minnette Carpenter,
Mary Jo Brantley,
Cissie McCampbell,
Lucille Terry
Excelsior House

Chuck and Patsy Watts
Vagabond House

Lowell and Barbara Bogart
James House

Bob Cote
Tanque Verde Ranch

11

recreational facilities in the Cascade Mountains. The imposing building stands today complete with art works, furniture and hand-forged hardware, the treasure trove of an era, all kept in good order by innkeeper Richard Kohnstamm. Guests get the benefit not only of the spectacular natural environment, but of the achievements of a not-so-distant generation of American artisans.

Also during the depression, Mrs. Isabella Greenway required a market for the western-style furniture produced by her handicraft workshops, since sales were almost nonexistent. The Arizona Inn was the answer, and its graciousness has been maintained by manager Robert Minerich, working with Mrs. Greenway's son John.

There are also innkeepers who pursue their trade with such spirit that they have become as legendary as their inns. L. D. Dennen, proprietor of the low-keyed Heritage House, near Mendocino, is one. He is on hand every day in the dining room for breakfast and dinner. "People expect to see me," he says. A natty dresser with a slightly mischievous smile, he loves the particulars of attending ever so subtly to people's needs, and seems both proud and slightly surprised at the way Heritage House has developed. He is particularly enthusiastic

Leif Benson
Eric Black
Rosemary Campiformio
Richard Wasserman
Ted Black
St. Orres

Dorene Musilli
Sonoma Hotel

about the young innkeepers who are "coming up," many of whom he has helped with advice and interest. Ned Smith, of St. Helena's Wine Country Inn has called him the dean of California's innkeepers. One can hear Don Dennen sweetly protesting that he never thought of himself as academic.

Innkeeper Dick Langdon has a distinctly different style. His Union Hotel at Los Alamos shows his love for the florid and the outre. His hotel has a vibrant energy that is a reflection of its creator. But it's also a place to relax—the organized recreation goes no farther than a thrown-together game of pool. Dick's furniture is fancy, and his style is lavish, but his philosophy is simple and direct. "A country inn," he explains, "is where you go to find out about yourself."

Mary and Bob Keenan
Burgundy House

Substantial investment.

Francis Wilcox James built this house for his retirement from active business. In designing it, he used an architectural pattern book published in New York, which the present owners recently bought at auction, together with James's diaries and his top hat.

JAMES HOUSE
Port Townsend, Washington

Port Townsend once hoped to become a great city. Founded in 1851 near the southern entrance to Puget Sound, by the 1880s it had become a bustling seaport. Ships from all over the world stood in the harbor, and most of the major maritime nations had consulates there. Merchants from Europe, lumbermen from the Pacific Northwest, seal hunters from Russia and American Indians from Washington coastal villages all mingled on the docks. Port Townsend could be a rough town, though. A farmhand could go into one of the dockside bars for a drink and wake up the next day with a terrific hangover and an unsolicited position on a ship bound for Macao.

For a time, Port Townsend, with its busy harbor and burgeoning industries, had dreams of becoming the Pittsburgh—or perhaps the New York—of the West. To fulfill its promise all the town needed was a rail link to a city inland. Land speculators moved in, anticipating boom times, and in 1890 a town of less than seven thousand recorded almost $5 million worth of real estate transactions.

Nothing was too grand for Port Townsend. In the lower town, near the wharves, elaborate office blocks of stone, brick and cast iron were erected. In the upper town, the leaders of the community threw up a score of sumptuous Victorian houses. Early in the '90s, though, the bubble of prosperity burst when the long-planned rail link was dropped.

The most substantial of the great houses was put up in 1889 by Francis Wilcox James. James may have been the richest man in town—his profession was listed in Port Townsend's 1890 *City Directory* simply as "Capitalist"— and his home advertised his great wealth. At a time when $4,000 was adequate to build a really fine home, James spent at least twice that amount. The foundation story, fashioned by

Treasure chambers.

The bridal suite boasts a spacious antechamber with a view of Port Townsend Bay. The patterned parquet floor contains a recess in which James kept a small metal box, presumably for the money he did not bank. The living room furniture is original to the house; it was discovered in the carriage house by Bill Eaton, the former innkeeper, during his restoration. Lowell Bogart enjoys telling ghost stories around the fire here late at night.

an English mason, was made entirely from imported bricks. The interior walls were given three separate coats of plaster. The stairway railings and balusters were of wild cherrywood brought from Virginia and finished in a beautiful spiral design by local craftsmen.

After Francis James died, his home went to seed. By the 1930s, it had become a none-too-respectable rooming house with its high ceilings lowered and fine rooms converted into cubbyholes. It stayed that way until the early 1960s, when Bill and Frances Eaton bought it and set to work on a massive restoration. Three years were devoted to reclaiming the spaces of the original rooms, another year to rewiring the house. Altogether, the Eatons spent nine years on the restoration. When they were finished, the James House had regained all its old luster.

The present owners, Lowell and Barbara Bogart, discovered the James House by accident. They had come to Port Townsend one rainy day in August, 1976, just to look around. Lowell had no experience as an innkeeper; he was a geologist from Oklahoma. But the desire to run an inn is the kind of passion that often strikes suddenly and deeply. "We slept in it one night," Lowell recalls, "and we owned the place the next day."

The Bogarts maintained the Eatons' high standards and added several graceful touches of their own. Barbara Bogart keeps a variety of beautiful plants in the house. They stand on pedestals and wrought-iron holders in the two expansively furnished parlors on the main floor, and are placed at windows in the bedrooms. There are ten guest rooms

17

A single rose

is the Bogarts' daily offering in the bridal suite. Couples celebrating a significant event are also likely to find champagne cooling in a silver bucket. Beautiful decorative touches abound. The shades of an early electric lamp, below, seem to have sprouted from the wallpaper behind.

at the James House. On the ground floor are the garden suites. One has a fireplace, a spool bed and a bed with a cane headboard that looks as if Ethel Barrymore might once have owned it.

The house has a number of decorating blockbusters upstairs. In one room is a carved Oriental sofa and two chairs with armrests in the shape of dragons. In another room is a brass-banded oak bedroom set with a carved acorn motif. But the most luxurious accommodation is the bridal suite, a full-blown Victorian extravaganza, whose furniture would have done Francis James proud. The bed has a magnificent headboard with panels of walnut burl. In the anteroom is a long red fainting couch, a Victorian rocker and an armchair placed in the four-window bay with a view out over Port Townsend.

A room with a view at the James House is no mean thing, for all around the town, across the water, rise high mountains, snow-capped through most of the year.

The ferry to Whidbey Island,

overleaf, leaves from Port Townsend's lower town, where relics of the 1880s boom still stand. Beyond the island rise the peaks of the North Cascades. To the south and west of town are the Olympics; to the east, Mount Rainier.

Period pieces.

The Garland stove, right, from one of the garden suites, has a humidifier in the shape of an urn at its top. The delicately tinted glass of a panel in the dining room, below, caught the Bogarts' eye at an auction. It fits beautifully with the beveled and leaded glass already in the house.

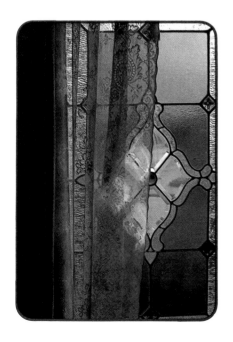

At the James house, amid enthusiastic talk about the town, breakfast is served each day in the kitchen, where guests gather around an oak table in front of a big iron cookstove that Barbara keeps busy all morning. The Bogarts serve a dozen different kinds of homemade bread, including apricot, anise bread and a three-grain loaf. Lowell toasts thick pieces for guests and hands around butter and his own homemade pear preserves. People like to linger over coffee, while Barbara acts as social director and makes sure that all the guests are introduced to one another.

At Port Townsend, one begins not only to understand the great dreams of the first developers, but to credit the restorers for their fidelity to what the nineteenth century achieved. Thanks to the high standards of the Eatons and the Bogarts, the James House is once again the finest home in town.

Natural resources.

Up the Captain Whidbey's madrona log staircase, left, a bright band of windows lights the inn's well-stocked library. Innkeeper Steve Stone keeps its selection of popular novels, literary classics and non-fiction up-to-date. The long, low line of the inn, above, faces the water of Penn Cove. A painted detail from an old sea chest, inset, recalls Whidbey Island's seafaring heritage.

THE CAPTAIN WHIDBEY

Coupeville, Washington

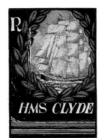

Some people are just naturally stubborn and want to do things the hard way no matter how much trouble it is. Judge Lester Still must have been such a man. The local magistrate on Whidbey Island in Puget Sound around the turn of the century, Judge Still laid out his plans for a summer resort hotel in 1907 and had it built entirely of madrona logs. The madrona tree is lovely to look at but difficult to work with. Its bark peels back to reveal a reddish wood that, when dried, is harder to cut than steel. The tree grows in a twisted, angular fashion that makes it hard to find logs straight enough to build with easily. But the madrona trees were indigenous and the judge liked them—so madrona it was.

The inn was popular from the start, and summer vacationers came sailing over from Tacoma and Seattle to tie up at the judge's personal dock on Penn Cove. Then, as now, Whidbey island was a quiet place for relaxing and soaking up a bit of history.

The area's first white settler, Thomas Glasgow, arrived in 1848 but

Rustic fantasy.

The Captain Whidbey's living room has comfort and character. The portrait over the mantel is of the innkeeper's grandmother as a girl. The gigantic fireplace and the virtuoso structure of the ceiling were probably designed to impress guests up from Seattle on the paddle-steamer with the picturesqueness of this part of the country.

Room for repose.

The afternoon sun warms the porch of the inn's new building, designed to keep the spirit of the old lodge.

was driven away by hostile Skagit Indians. Issac Ebey then led a new party of pioneers to the island. The new colony was none too easy about its relations with local Indians. In 1855 the settlers built a series of blockhouses to protect their homes, one of which still remains. Although the blockhouses helped the settlement survive, they weren't enough to save Issac Ebey. One day in 1857, a war party of Haida Indians stormed onto the island and killed Mr. Ebey. A stone marker commemorating his death stands near Ebey's Landing.

There are several historic houses on the island, but few are as interesting as the rustic lodge that is the Captain Whidbey Inn, named for Captain Joseph Whidbey, who first sailed through Deception Pass in 1792. The public rooms and most of the bedrooms and cottages have sparkling marine views, often with awesome glimpses of the Cascade Mountains beyond, on the mainland.

The rooms at the inn are generally short on space but long on rustic charm. They are furnished with local pieces, and all have handsome marble-topped wash basins. The adjoining cottages are somewhat larger, with their own sitting rooms and fireplaces. Across the property, on a small inlet off Penn Cove, are the Lagoon buildings. These contain spacious rooms with private baths, usually a chest or a table that has a little age on it, and a view of the bucolic shores that surround Whidbey, an island with a heritage not only of seafaring men but of farmers and loggers as well.

Now accessible by both bridge and ferry, the Captain Whidbey is

Arbutus alcove.

Arbutus is another name for the madrona tree, whose wood forms the walls and ceilings of the corner suite, below, where guests can hear the gentle lap of water in the cove and the murmur of the breeze through the ancient firs in the grove around the inn.

25

Dutch touch.

Portents of spring, these cut tulips decorate a table in the Captain Whidbey's dining room, where diners enjoy the pleasant, relaxed atmosphere.

The Chart Room,

where boisterous boaters and landlubbers alike meet to converse, carouse and kid. A woman bartender is traditional at the inn. Bottles are inscribed with names, dates and occasions; business cards paper the walls and ceiling.

27

only ninety minutes from Seattle and has become a popular year-round restaurant. The Chart Room, an extremely active cocktail lounge, is furnished in a happy jumble of artifacts. Hundreds of old bottles hang from the ceiling rafters, along with a Canton flag from Switzerland that is draped like a tent over part of the room.

The dining room is cheerful, with windows all along the wall that overlooks the cove. Seafood is naturally a specialty of the house, but four times a year there is a special dinner party. In February, it's a Chinese New Year spectacular; in April, it's "April in Paris," with a special French gourmet meal; the Oktoberfest is properly celebrated with stout German food; and for Christmas, there is a traditional English holiday meal with baked oysters, oxtail soup and a fine fat goose that Charles Dickens's Tiny Tim would have loved. This banquet is so popular that it is now served twice a year.

The present owners of the Captain Whidbey Inn are the Stone family. Steve Stone, a retired army captain from Massachusetts, and his wife Shirlee took over in 1964. It is very much a family-run establishment. Mrs. Stone once did all the cooking, but she now limits herself mostly to preparing the special dinners that have made the inn so popular. Sons John and Geoff are very active at the inn and are starting to take over more and more of its management. As a result, Steve now happily claims that he is semiretired. "Nowadays," he explains, "I don't have to work more than eight or ten hours a day."

28

TIMBERLINE LODGE
Government Camp, Oregon

High class.

A ski class at Timberline, seen through a window of the lodge. A ski resort built 6,000 feet up Mount Hood, Oregon's highest peak, Timberline was a WPA project begun to demonstrate the indomitable spirit of the state's people. Among the lodge's many art works is the glass mosaic in the Paul Bunyan Bar, inset. Although the lodge operates year-round, it is at its most spectacular when buried in snow and ice, as shown above and *overleaf.* Heidi, below, is the lodge's social director and resident paramedic.

When President Franklin D. Roosevelt dedicated this impressive ski lodge at the timber line, six thousand feet up on Mount Hood, he called it "a monument to the skill and faithful performance of workers."

Timberline is the result of a unique public works project. Its building began in 1935, in the depth of the Great Depression, when hundreds of unemployed men were put to work by the Works Progress Administration and the Civilian Conservation Corps, clearing land and constructing the lodge.

European stonemasons were brought in to teach unskilled Americans their craft. Together, they took some four hundred tons of volcanic stones from nearby canyons, chiseled them into shape and lifted them into place to make the central fireplace with its chimney nearly one hundred feet high. The huge Ponderosa pine pillars that support the roof of the central space were cut in nearby forests, then hand-hewn by broadax and smoothed by adz. By the 1930s blacksmithing was virtually a lost art, but under the direction of a master smith, the men learned it and created a unique collection of handwrought gates, light fixtures, ornaments and hardware for the lodge. Conceived in a simple but massive style, the furniture was constructed with strap iron; chairs and bench seats were made out of laced rawhide; chair backs and tabletops were crafted from thick hardwood planks. When the workmen were finished, they literally gave the shirts off their backs to help finish the work. The lodge needed more than one hundred hooked rugs to decorate the rooms; most of them were made by Oregon women from the worn-out blankets and uniforms of CCC workmen.

Three hundred sixty feet long, four stories high and topped by a

On the wing.

In a recently completed addition to the lodge, this sheet-metal sculpture of ravens on the wing decorates the Raven's Nest Lounge.

A style to match the mountain.

The furniture at Timberline is massive, as is the building itself. A balustrade of sawed-off telephone poles borders the Ram's Head Bar, left, and forms a balcony around the lobby, at whose center is the grandiose chimney, *overleaf*. At ground level, the same chimney warms skiers chilled from a day on the slopes.

750-pound brass and bronze weather vane, Timberline cost almost $1 million. It could not be duplicated today for twenty times that much. Richard Kohnstamm, who has run the lodge for the past twenty-two years, notes that Oregon people regard it with great respect. Most of those who visit, he says, have at least one family member—an uncle, a brother, a grandmother—who worked on the project.

At Timberline today, a guest can only marvel at how much durable beauty was created by relatively unskilled labor. The lobby is a room the size of a small cathedral. On the heavy wooden staircases, the newel posts are made from cedar utility poles, each carved on top in the shape of a native bird or animal. At the head of the front staircase, a huge door, with fittings so impressive they would make a Norseman blink, opens onto a balcony offering a sweeping view of Mount Hood's

forested slopes, the valley far below and the peak of Mount Jefferson forty miles to the south.

The fifty bedrooms are furnished with pieces especially designed for the lodge. While those in the public rooms are only vaguely reminiscent of Art Deco, the bedrooms are a clear reflection of that style, popular in the years the lodge was built. Especially interesting are the corner desks of blond wood, all angles, placed in several rooms. Since the lodge serves skiers, the fact that the furniture is massive and indestructible helps; but Kohnstamm was concerned that the designs for rugs, draperies and bedspreads would be lost, so he and other Oregonians organized Friends of Timberline, a group that is restoring many of Timberline's rooms to their original state.

Timberline's skiing has been considered among the finest in the world ever since a group of sportsmen from Portland first broke snow trails here in 1906. On a busy weekend, thousands of skiers pass through the lodge's ski facilities in the lower lobby on the way to the slopes. Mount Hood attracts climbers, as well as skiers. The highest peak in Oregon at 11,235 feet, it was first scaled in 1857 and is now the most popular snowcapped mountain climb in the Northern Hemisphere.

The Blue Gentian Room

is only one of many at Timberline recently restored by Friends of Timberline. New appliquéd draperies and bedspreads were made and new rugs hooked, all to the original designs of the 1930s.

Courtyard bazaar.

A pottery display in the courtyard of the inn's Long House conference center. Salishan has its own art gallery, where it shows Oregon artists, and the inn's rooms house a fine collection of native Oregon art.

Native to the place.

In the Attic Lounge, the huge fireplace of native stone and the wall, shingled in a traditional Oregon pattern, emphasize the inn's close connection with local building practice. The globes of the chandelier are glass floats from Japan, gathered on nearby Oregon beaches.

SALISHAN LODGE

Gleneden Beach, Oregon

The coastline of northern Oregon is an area of awesome natural beauty, with unspoiled beaches and high capes thrusting out into the ocean. Huge offshore rocks are whipped by winds and spray. The whole strand has a timeless, primeval quality. The surprise is not that this particular stretch of coastline became the family playground of Oregon but that the area could have been developed with such a meticulous eye for the delicate balances of nature. There are, of course, a few mindless, honky-tonk beach resorts along the way; however, there is also Salishan Lodge, an absolutely modern resort hotel with golf courses, tennis courts and facilities for small conventions.

Care for the environment is visible everywhere at Salishan. The lodge's 150 guest accommodations are all attached to the main building by a series of covered walkways, but the guests have the feeling of being tucked away in a setting of natural wilderness, where the ocean, although not seen, is sensed, just over the next rise. All guest rooms have elegant brick fireplaces and mammoth baths; all accommodations are as spacious as the West. Constructed from native Douglas fir and cedar, they are rugged rooms; yet they have touches of luxury and elegance. All the rooms contain contemporary artwork by Oregon artists, and almost all the rooms have their own balconies for admiring the incredible scenic beauty.

The interiors of the public rooms in the main lodge are studies in contrasts, combining light and dark, intimacy and grandeur. A fine attention to detail and a rugged stone fireplace bring what could have been an almost intimidatingly large lobby down to manageable proportions.

The Gourmet Dining Room at Salishan has an international reputa-

Giant trees, *overleaf,* brought down the rivers during storms, are often flung back onto Oregon's beaches as driftwood.

Outside in.

The formal setting of the Gourmet Dining Room is enclosed by a sweeping panorama of greenery, bay and distant ocean. Salishan's respect for the natural does not inhibit civilized delight; the menu is international in scope, fine in quality.

tion. In an imposing room built on three levels, the emphasis of the décor is on blending with nature. Finished in natural woods, the room has windows everywhere to let diners enjoy the view of Siletz Bay and the ocean beyond. Their first time here, most guests gorge themselves on salmon. Salishan is famous for its salmon barbecues, where the chef prepares whole, standing sides of salmon around an open charcoal grate. Seafood is a specialty of the house, from filet of sole Marguery, with tiny shrimp in a delicate cream sauce, to the delicious *coulibiac,* a filet of Chinook salmon layered with mushrooms, rice, onion and shrimp, and baked in a puff pastry. The menu goes on for some nine pages, offering a full range of international cuisine. In fact, if guests will give chef Franz Buck forty-eight hours notice, he will specially prepare anything they want from the cuisines of virtually any country.

Whether the guests are a family coming for the weekend, or a small group of businessmen coming for a quiet conference, recreation at Salishan is built around enjoyment of the outdoors in the Oregon coastal region. There are indoor and outdoor tennis courts, an indoor swimming pool and an eighteen-hole, oceanside, championship golf course with some of the most scenic fairways in the country. Fishing, naturally, is a major activity, with rock and surf fishing in nearby Fogarty Creek State Park and Siletz Bay. Unexcelled deep-sea fishing is available five miles south of Salishan, by sailing out from Depoe Bay, one of the most picturesque villages on the Pacific coast. Many of the guests, however, don't bother with such organized activities; just walking around the area is enough to satisfy some. Salishan Lodge is

42

Incidentally Oriental.

A tradition of Japanese-style gardening is strong in Oregon, and nowhere more evident than at Salishan Lodge. A pavilion at the main lodge, upper left, is stylistically linked to Japanese palaces, despite its board-and-batten siding; and the carefully trimmed shrubbery bespeaks an Oriental model. The light well between two sections of roof, right, is a signature element in the work of architect John Storrs.

part of an 800-acre preserve with trails through it. It has printed up its own botanical guide with detailed descriptions of the forty-five different species of plants that grow there. Three miles down the road between the ocean and Siletz Bay is a sand spit where huge pieces of driftwood are piled, their grotesque shapes forming a monumental garden in the sand. Herds of sea lions can be seen from the beach, and occasionally a glass net float will make the journey all the way from Yokohama and wash up on the shore.

There is an abundance of blue herons on the bay, and Salishan is a favorite spot for birdwatchers. The lodge also employs a knowledgeable guide to lead children on nature walks.

Salishan Lodge demonstrates that it is possible to live close to nature, in a splendid setting, and yet forfeit none of the joys of civilization. If it is ostentatious at all, Salishan errs on the side of the angels. In the evening, the outside lights are kept very low so the guests can better enjoy looking up at the stars. At Salishan, stargazing is a major spectator sport.

44

Geological spectacular.

These rock formations are survivors of the battering sea that rolls in constantly, undercutting the cliffs on which Mendocino stands. The Mendocino headlands, now a state park, are just a short walk from Main Street.

MacCALLUM HOUSE

Mendocino, California

45

Bed and breakfast.

With a breakfast of hot millet bread, juice and coffee served to the bedroom, it's hard not to start the day well. Inset is the inn's front door.

For years, whenever a Hollywood studio wanted a location shooting for a small New England town but didn't have the time or the money to send a crew across the country, it would dispatch one to Mendocino. Perched on cliffs some fifty feet above the Pacific Ocean, a four-hour drive north from San Francisco, Mendocino can still pass for a rugged little New England coastal village. The loggers who came here in the 1850s to cut down the stand of giant redwoods by Big River were mostly from New England and Nova Scotia, and they brought their own ideas of how a proper town should look, such as: precise, practical, plain and pretty all at the same time.

One of the gems of this kind of transplanted architecture is the MacCallum House, built in 1882 by William H. Kelley as a wedding present for his newly married daughter Daisy MacCallum. The house, one of the finest residences in the community, was for many years the center of Mendocino social life. In 1974, the old place, with all its furnishings, was purchased by Bill and Sue Norris of San Francisco, who set to work converting it into a country inn and restaurant. No renovation is really easy, but the well-kept house, looked after by caretakers for years after the MacCallums had left, saved Bill and Sue many headaches. Most of the original rooms remain intact, but one modern addition is a marvelous bar, handmade from golden and California oak. Bill commissioned the bar from a local carpenter, who came and measured the area and then disappeared for months. He reappeared only days before the official opening of the inn to install the bar. Every piece fit perfectly. That is the way of the MacCallum House: everything fits perfectly.

The rooms upstairs are pleasant examples of "the way folks used to

A family picture

sits on a table in the redwood paneled upstairs hall. Mrs. MacCallum's library, upper right, now serves as the inn's restaurant.

Sun spot.

The sun porch in the Grey Whale Bar is a perfect setting for a late-afternoon glass of wine from one of the Mendocino County vineyards. The macramé curtain is a recent addition, but many of the furnishings date from the inn's days as a private home.

live." They remind more than one guest of the house of a grandmother, or perhaps a favorite aunt, where they spent weekends as a child. Among the six bedrooms on the second floor, one features a charming French sleigh bed, brass door fittings and a rocker by the window with a view of the town. Another bedroom is furnished with white wicker furniture in the style of the 1920s, which looks delightful with the bright new wallpaper Sue has chosen.

The third floor is the attic, which has been converted into a set of marvelously cozy rooms. Its hall is lined with trunks still brimming with memorabilia of Daisy MacCallum, whose long life in the house ended only in the 1950s. The walls are papered with pages from newspaper rotogravure sections from the early 1900s, giving guests a pleasant and informal grounding in the social history of an earlier America.

Around the inn are several outbuildings that have been converted into distinctive guest accommodations. The Greenhouse has been transformed into a snug, rustic cottage with its own fireplace. Rooms are available, too, in the newly renovated Carriage House, which has five bedrooms and a sleeping loft for children. From the huge window in the upstairs living room, guests can see the waves crashing up against the rocks in the cove below. Many couples enjoy the fantasy of staying in the Gazebo, a converted children's playhouse nestled in a bed of geraniums. The room is small, but the bed is definitely large enough for adults.

The MacCallum House's restaurant, in the main house, is a set of friendly rooms with ceilings paneled in dark-stained tongue-and-groove and walls lined with bookshelves containing Daisy MacCallum's extensive library, strong in books on travel and religion. The restaurant has a Continental menu and serves a piquant variety of veal, lamb and seafood dishes at tables lit by kerosene lamps. It is generally considered to serve the best food in town.

Bill and Sue are both transplanted easterners. He is a stockbroker in

Rough equivalents.

Despite a similarity in texture, the pictures at right are of two different buildings. The rustic attic parlor is in the main house; the picture at top shows the spruced-up exterior of the Carriage House, which contains five luxurious bedrooms.

Clapboard castle.

The small cottage of the 1880s was enlarged in 1908 and moved to get a better view of the bay. The redwood bedroom at left is palatial and features a sleigh bed and an elaborate French commode.

Overleaf: the town of Mendocino at sunset.

San Francisco but originally comes from New England, where he summered on Nantucket for years. According to Bill, Mendocino is very much a Nantucket-on-the-Pacific, an ideal community in a splendid natural setting, populated with a concerned citizenry trying to live in accord with nature. Mendocino also shares the fiercely independent spirit of Nantucket Islanders and has steadfastly refused to put in city water. They still rely on individual wells, because they feel that if they had city water, commercial development would not be far behind.

Many of the townspeople are also in the forefront of the fight to save the great whales. As a sort of bow to the struggle, the Norrises have named their bar the Grey Whale; and a large sculpture of a whale by Byrd Baker, a local artist involved in the movement, stands on the front lawn. Mendocino independence is almost always partly a matter of an artist's independence as well, since many artists live in town. Feelings run high, and outrage over some issues a few years ago led a group from Mendocino to secede from California to form their own state. In a sense, Mendocino is its own state, since its physical beauty and isolation, combined with its newly acquired cultural life, lead to a distinctive and refreshing state of mind. Visitors to the MacCallum House are privy to it all.

View of the cove below the inn.

HERITAGE HOUSE
Little River, California

Relic and type.

The front door of Heritage House, a farmhouse built by John Dennen, innkeeper L. D. Dennen's grandfather. Today the door opens not only to the original house, but into a long dining room with a panoramic view of the turbulent cove and the ocean beyond. The inset shows a stained-glass Art Nouveau tulip.

For such an elegant establishment, Heritage House has had an unusually racy past. The original farmhouse was built in 1877 for Wilder Pullen, a lumberman who used the site as a shipping point for transporting handsplit redwood ties. But the rough seas and irregular coastline of Pullen's Landing eventually came to have less honorable uses. The rocky cove at the base of the cliffs was a smugglers' haven. Illegal aliens, mostly Asians used as a source of cheap labor for building the railroads in the late 1800s, were regularly slipped ashore by the boatload. During Prohibition, the cove was practically a marina for rumrunners. Baby Face Nelson once used the farmhouse as a hideout.

Innkeeper L.D. Dennen was visiting the area in 1949 when he found the house. His grandfather had built it for the Pullen family, and the building, though battered and abandoned, still retained the graceful lines and fine craftsmanship of the "State of Maine" architecture typical of the northern California coast at that time. And then there was the site; on a coast where spectacular ocean views are commonplace, the property had an unmatched panorama of cliffs, cove, rocks and ocean. Don Dennen recalls that arrangements for buying the place were "made within the hour," and he and his wife set about creating Heritage House.

The original house has been combined with other structures to provide a nucleus for the inn. The interiors are a masterful combination of theatrical effects and creature comforts. The lounge was originally an apple storage house that Dennen discovered twenty-four miles away. He had it disassembled, carted over the road and put back together again on his property. The lounge is a spacious, heavy-beamed room with round oak tables, comfortable easy chairs and a huge fireplace.

Saturday spectacular.

A display of gleaming copper is part of the panoply of Heritage House's Saturday night buffet. At this Mendocino social event, prime rib is featured, but the kitchen prepares an almost unending variety of special salads as well.

But at Heritage House, no surface is without its touch of luxury: the rustic ceilings are illuminated by elegant crystal chandeliers.

Between the original house and the lounge is the long, wide, window-walled dining room, which overlooks the spectacle of the rocky cove. A modern room with subdued old-fashioned elegance, its tables set with butter-yellow linen, classic white china, and flowers from the Heritage House gardens, the dining room more than equals the lounge as a center of social life at the inn.

The aim of the kitchen is to produce good, well-prepared American food rather than an elevated Continental cuisine, and it is grandly realized. Of the soups, the cream of mushroom is rich but delicate; the cream of celery, smooth as silk. There are beautifully presented appetizers, such as pear almondine. Two entrées are offered each night, one of fish, usually in a distinctive sauce, and a meat dish, often served with garnishes and ingredients that contrast the hearty with the sweet—a ginger-glazed corned beef, a pork chop Polynesian, for example. Desserts are sedate but luxurious—lovely tortes and parfaits, even a hot fudge sundae. The food, the smooth civility of the service and the attention to leisurely dining to be enjoyed as one of life's best experiences make a dinner at Heritage House special.

Breakfast in the sun-struck dining room is equally pleasant. Guests begin at the buffet set up in a skylighted alcove, where they may help themselves to a variety of juices and fruits in syrup—pears, peaches, figs, rhubarb.

Back at their tables, they are served their choice of hot dishes from the kitchen—usually ham, bacon, sausage and hash are available, and eggs done in any style. Also popular are the silver-dollar-size hotcakes, made from a special house recipe developed by Mrs. Dennen. They are so light, Don Dennen declares, "you don't chew them, you crush them with your tongue." Guests prepare toast at their tables, each one of which has its own toaster, to do personal justice to Heritage House's great variety of home-baked breads.

Although there are a few guest rooms in the main building, most of

55

Matutinal repast.

The full breakfast served is a leisurely one, with toasters at each table, and a wide variety of fruits and juices available at the buffet. The long line of windows in the picture at left, forms the back wall of Heritage House's bar.

Cottages are placed on the
carefully landscaped
grounds so that they do
not block one another's
view. The unit at right is
roofed with sod.

Mendocino's heritage

is recalled in the names of the buildings at Heritage House. Above is Stable, with a decorative birdhouse cupola. The simple exteriors conceal luxurious rooms with wide beds, soft carpets and local antiques.

April in February.

Alders in bud near the duckpond, and flowers in profusion throughout the grounds announce the arrival of spring well before it comes to more dreary parts of the world.

the accommodations are in cottages tucked away on the hillside. "We've given them names inspired by the early-day buildings of the area," Dennen explains. One of the favorites is called "Scott's Opera House," which was a center of entertainment on the coast for traveling minstrel shows. This unit features a hand-cranked motion-picture machine Don's grandfather won in a poker game. To keep the lodging units unobtrusive in the landscape, Dennen has in one case gone the limit by imitating a "sod buster's" home: the roof is covered by turf which resembles a stretch of ground like any other.

As Heritage House has grown, the new accommodations have tended to become more spacious, and luxurious. "We try to put really interesting furniture in the rooms. Many of the pieces have been made by local carpenters, and many more came around the Horn and up to Little River by schooner." Typical of the larger units is La Maison 2, situated high on the hill, with a view of the ocean and the outer cliffs of the cove. A huge room with two queen-size beds and French Provincial and Sheraton furniture, it resembles an elegant suite at the Plaza Hotel. Few hotel suites of this kind, however, are found in a secluded cottage at the restless edge of a boundless sea. Another unit, the Water Tower—it really *was* a water tower—is a spectacular duplex with a two-story living room and a sleeping balcony.

Almost any country inn represents a retreat from the world outside; usually it is a retreat to a simpler way of life. At Heritage House, it is a retreat to luxury.

A rich reception.

Stained-glass windows by Saum Hawley in doors of California oak form one wall of the inn's reception area. The Art Nouveau cabinet and Edwardian furniture seem right at home.

Extravagant by nature.

The dining room tower, with its stained-glass windows and octagonal dome, provides an exotic setting for sophisticated food at St. Orres. The patterned linen napkins are drawn through thick copper napkin rings that are actually plumber's pipe sleeves. Meals are served on stoneware thrown by a local potter.

Displaced dacha.

Eric Black, the designer of St. Orres, is proud that much of the inn, *overleaf*, was built of "scrounged" materials. These include the copper sheathing of the domes, made from the discarded cladding of computer control equipment.

ST. ORRES

Gualala, California

The St. Orres is as much a triumph of the spirit as it is of design. Its antic array of ornate domes is not, as one might expect, the work of nineteenth-century Russian craftsmen. It is the creation of a pair of young, contemporary American master carpenters, who put the place together, piece by piece. Richard Wasserman and Eric Black bought a dilapidated guest house and went to work building their own place around it. They were influenced by buildings constructed by Russian trappers on California's coast in the nineteenth century, but their final creation went far beyond any frontier house. St. Orres is a place of rare architectural distinction.

As do all good carpenters, Richard and Eric love the feel of a fine piece of wood. Inside, all the rooms are lined with tongue-and-groove redwood, while the outside of the inn is clad in Oregon red cedar. When they found that an old sawmill framed with heavy timber was going to close in Philo, an inland town up the coast, they assembled their friends and salvaged all of the mill they could, dismantling it and moving the beams to Gualala, where they used them to frame their own inn. Costs were not important, only quality. When they occasionally ran out of money, they simply stopped work, moved into mountain cabins and lived off the land.

By 1977, Richard and Eric were finally able to open one of the most unusual inns in the West, one that was not constructed in the usual sense but built by hand, room by room.

St. Orres is filled with a series of stunning effects. A massive stone fireplace, its mantel made from a cleanly cut fir beam, takes up more than half the inside wall of the first-floor sitting room and stands opposite six California oak doors, placed side by side, each with its

61

own locally made stained-glass window. The dining room, ending in a domed tower, soars a full three stories. The eight bedrooms upstairs all have built-in beds and walls of the redwood tongue-and-groove in striking geometric designs. Each room has a specially designed storage cabinet, combining both chest and wardrobe. The shelves in the kitchen would be the envy of most fine cabinetmakers, and at St. Orres even the telephone booth is lined in redwood.

Amidst this natural opulence, the focus is on the restaurant. Chef Leif Benson produces an excellent Continental Cuisine, often prepared with a touch more piquancy and texture than is traditional. His apt use of seasonings and vegetables is part of the explanation. Spanish lentil soup at St. Orres has a clarity and tartness both bracing and delicate. Chef Benson, at the age of 24, knows how to treat his ingredients with respect. Côte de veau Maintenon is a fragrant, succulent triumph. The veal chop is sautéed in butter, baked with a purée of rice and onions, then topped with a gorgeous julienne of ham and mushrooms. Vegetables are audacious and delicious—a buttery, eye-startling mix of

Redwood revival.

Each of the eight bedrooms has a freely designed wall made from the replaned redwood tongue-and-groove of the old structure. The elaborate velvet quilts are made by Anne Kessler of Point Arena. The inn's intricate logo is inscribed on the door of the skylighted double shower. The hallways are skylighted as well.

carrots with tender asparagus, for example. Desserts overload all circuits; there is a chocolate decadence, its name warning the unwary. For overnight guests the complimentary morning meal is a spread of fresh grapefruit, locally made cakes and pastries, juice, nuts, raisins and large bowls of yogurt, served with coffee and a variety of teas.

Many guests come only for the food, making the long drive north from San Francisco along the winding coast. Others come for St. Orres' isolation and wonderful natural setting. Waves crash spectacularly against the rocks in the craggy cove opposite the inn. The inn's beach, next cove up, is a protected curve of sand at the mouth of the creek. St. Orres' thirty-five acres, forested with redwoods, run back into the hills above the shore. Eventually, Eric, Richard and their friends will build cabins for the inn within the shelter of this coastal forest. They know that to do things well takes time and care, though. St. Orres is a special place, and these carpenter-innkeepers move with the deliberateness of mature imaginations. No one plans to rush things.

66

Plaza suite.

The hotel is located at one corner of the plaza of Sonoma, laid out by the Mexicans who settled the area. A second-floor balcony, since lost, was a favorite place to view the annual vintage festival. The Musillis plan to restore it.

SONOMA HOTEL

Sonoma, California

Sonoma County lays claim to the status of "cradle of California history" with considerable justification. Barely a yard of this area is untouched by the state's early social and political history. Russian, English, Mexican, Spanish and American flags have flown over the region. Mission San Francisco Solano, the northernmost of the California missions, was established in 1823. For a dozen years it was just a sleepy, distant outpost of the Mexican empire. Then, to counter the incursion of the Russians, who had built a fort less than one hundred miles from San Francisco, the governor of Alta California ordered an energetic young officer, Mariano Guadalupe Vallejo, to take a detachment of cavalry and establish military outposts in the area. Vallejo did so well that he was later ordered to found a town at Mission San Francisco Solano. At the mission, he laid out the plaza that is now the town square.

As it turned out, there was little to fear from the tiny Russian colony. When the real trouble came, it was from the American trappers and traders who were pushing west across the Rockies. In a bloodless coup in June, 1846, a group of them seized the town from Mexico and raised the Bear Flag, proclaiming the land to be an independent republic. At the end of the Mexican War, in 1848, the area was annexed with the rest of California by the United States.

Another revolution, somewhat quieter but almost equally important, took place in 1855 when Hungarian nobleman Agoston Haraszthy came to Sonoma. Haraszthy had spent ten years crossing the new continent in search of a wineland comparable to the soil of his homeland and finally found what he was looking for in Sonoma. He bought five hundred acres just east of town and planted them with vine cuttings of varietal grapes from Europe. Fired with optimism over the oppor-

Big brass bend.

Innkeeper Dorene Musilli decided that the major brass bed at the Sonoma Hotel would have to be a beauty. It dominates Room 1.

tunities in his adopted country, Haraszthy built a stone winery in the Sonoma foothills, and the California wine industry was born.

Nobody is exactly sure when the hotel was built, but it has been dated as early as 1872. At various times it served as the town bar, a boarding house, a meeting hall and a dry goods store. Around 1920, the owners of the Sebastiani Winery bought it and converted it into the Plaza Hotel. The present owners, John and Dorene Musilli, bought it in 1974 and set about restoring and refurnishing the hotel in a nineteenth-century style. The frame building, with adobe infill, was structurally sound and the Musillis had to do very little in the way of basic alterations, although the woodwork had to be stripped of eight coats of paint before it could be brought back to its original luster.

All of the hotel's seventeen bedrooms are furnished with authentic items from the days of the Barbary Coast and the Gay Nineties. Perhaps the most impressive is Room 3, the Vallejo Room, which is furnished with pieces that once belonged to the general and his family. The bedroom suite, on loan from the Sonoma League for Historic Preservation, is a truly breathtaking set of matching Italianate pieces.

Many of the other rooms, while not quite so dramatic, are equally charming. Room 2 is a delightful bedroom with a five-piece handcarved suite topped with a rare orange marble. Room 6 has a unique bedroom set of solid oak inlaid with ebony and an unusual armoire with side shelves that looks like an Edwardian precursor of Art Deco. An adjoining antechamber with a small brass bed can accommodate a third

Heart of the West.

A Continental breakfast, served in the inn's lobby, features fresh coffee, warm croissants and lots of butter and jam.

Solar energy.

Sunlight filters through the lobby curtains. The etched-glass design on the front door, below right, lends a western feeling. The historic district adjacent to the plaza is a very pleasant place to stroll.

person. Room 29 features an enchanting pair of handcarved Austrian children's beds, a French dresser with its original tin mirror and a graceful chandelier.

The main sitting room downstairs is a warm gathering place with softly glowing woodwork illuminated by light from the splendid windows that look out onto the Sonoma plaza. In the morning, the lobby becomes a delightful setting for the hotel's Continental breakfast of coffee, croissants and jam.

The hotel has a wonderful asset in the person of manager Mianna Haraszthy, a delightful lady married to a descendant of the original Agoston Haraszthy, the father of California viniculture. Mrs. Haraszthy is especially helpful in suggesting day trips throughout the historic wine country. There are nearly a dozen wineries within a half hour's drive of the Sonoma Hotel.

The adobe relics of early Sonoma are everywhere around the plaza. The mission can be visited on one corner, and along the north side are buildings of the Sonoma State Historic Park, including the Mexican Soldiers' Barracks and the restored but nonfunctioning Hotel Toscano. The Toscano is not the only old hotel building in town, though. Down the street is the two-story adobe Blue Wing Inn, which now houses antiques shops. Built in 1840 by General Vallejo, the establishment has an impressive guest register that shows visits from such personalities of the Wild West as John C. Frémont, Kit Carson and the bandit Joaquin Murietta.

A pair of interesting sights from the world of literature can also be seen in the area. Jack London made his home in nearby Glen Ellen, which is now the Jack London State Historic Park. The ruins of his home, Wolf House, and his widow's home, The House of Happy Walls, containing mementos of London's meteoric career, are open to the public.

For contemporary literary interest, however, a guest need go no further than Room 21 back at the hotel. It was here that Maya Angelou wrote her novel *Singin' and Swingin' and Gettin' Merry Like Christmas.* The Sonoma Hotel is a great favorite of the author, who claims she will never be able to write another book there. "The room," she explains, "is just too beautiful to work in."

Worthy wood

forms the stairway, above, and adorns the Vallejo Room, opposite. The functional severity of the stairwell contrasts with the sumptuous rosewood of the bedroom set. The giant console lacks its crest; it would have made the piece too high for the room.

Unimpeachable sources.

The roofs of the inn take their form from the nineteenth-century styles of early Napa Valley buildings, the wineries and mills built by settlers from Europe.

WINE COUNTRY INN

St. Helena, California

Stone terraces lead downhill from this charming country inn to a patio edged with olive trees. A series of balconies extends out from the building, giving sweeping views of the valley and of the hills beyond. Chinese pistachios grow along the driveway, and even in January daisies bloom beside the exterior stairway. The Wine Country Inn looks as if it has long been part of the California landscape. The stone tower, the long walls of board and batten make one think of old barns or the outbuildings of some ancestral estate converted to a country house. It comes as a surprise to learn that the inn was only built in 1975.

73

Ned and Marge Smith had always wanted to be innkeepers, and for years they spent their vacations staying at inns in the British Isles, New England and the West, looking for ideas to incorporate into a place of their own. Finally, when they were clear about what they wanted, they built it from scratch. Instead of having an architect draw up the plans, they first went to an artist friend who sketched out what the place should look like. Then they designed the rooms to conform to the overall vision. They made each room different; if it didn't have its own balcony or its own patio, then it had to have some significant design feature all its own. It took a great deal of juggling to pull it off, but the result is an inn with all the style and intimacy of a nineteenth-century house, constructed with the sophisticated techniques and creature comforts of the twentieth century.

The common room of the inn is a large, comfortable area, paneled in rough-sawn barn siding, with red-flowered sofas and chairs drawn up in front of the large iron stove. Dominating the room is a long English harvest table, where breakfast is served to inn guests.

A line of oaks

runs along the edge of the drive up to the inn.

Each of the fourteen bedrooms is distinctively furnished and over half have fireplaces. One room has a solid Victorian bed that has been widened to accommodate a modern king-size mattress. Another is a perpetual Fourth of July celebration—a red carpet, an iron bedstead painted white and a blue wing chair in a cheerful room with red-white-and-blue striped wallpaper. Yet another room has two beds with headboards made of the bases of old wine casks. An American iron bed in one upstairs room is the least part of the decoration. A beautifully made quilt with a design of giant strawberries covers it. The upper walls of the room slope inward, following the lines of the mansard. High above, a pattern of strawberry plants winds across the paper of the rectangular panel of the ceiling.

Breakfast at Wine Country Inn consists of fruit, juice, coffee or tea, including a selection of herb teas, and a variety of hot breads. The inn serves no other meals, but there are a number of excellent restaurants

Founders and proprietors

Ned and Marge Smith worked actively on the construction and decoration of the inn. Ned and his son set the stone for the walls; Marge made many of the quilts that delight the inn's guests.

Keeping it simple.

The inn is designed with a refined but unaffected eye. Simple designs and simple materials form the background, as shown in the photo of a window, above. In contrast, the beds pull out all the decorative stops, as with the canopied extravaganza at right.

Napa Valley, January.

Mustard is grown as a cover crop on the valley floor, *overleaf,* to loosen the soil among the vines. In spring it will be turned under, when the vines begin to produce new growth. The vines in the foreground are veterans.

in St. Helena and throughout the Napa Valley. In fact, the Smiths waited to build their inn until the food available nearby was of sufficient quality to please their prospective guests. They'll make reservations for their guests, and they keep a collection of menus from local restaurants on the common room table. An especially pleasant touch in the common room is a cupboard well-stocked with wine glasses for guests' use. Guests are also free to chill their white wines in the inn's refrigerators. It's that kind of detail that makes up the rich heritage of gracious hospitality. After only three years, Ned and Marge Smith are already innkeepers in the classic mold.

**Cage
to catch
a dream.**
Innkeeper Mary Keenan
loves naive objects. At
right, one of her antique
French birdcages on a
table in the inn's
common room.

BURGUNDY HOUSE

Yountville, California

George Yount was an intrepid American pioneer, a frontiersman who settled in the Napa Valley in the 1830s on a vast tract of land given to him by Mariano Vallejo, the Mexican governor of Alta California. Yountville, the town that bears his name, was never a prepossessing place. Even today, it is a sleepy village where dogs snooze on front porches and vineyards grow right up to the houses. In the heart of Napa wine country, Yountville maintains the relaxed style of a century ago.

Charles Rouvegneau came to Yountville in 1870 and built a small, sturdy fieldstone house similar to the ones he remembered from his native France. Rouvegneau made wine on the first floor and rented out the rooms upstairs. The building served many purposes over the years, some respectable, some nefarious.

In 1975, Mary Keenan, a local antiques dealer, and her architect husband, Bob, took the place over as a shop. By then, the house had acquired a hundred years' worth of stucco, paint, plaster and assorted additions. Bob had everything sandblasted down to the original stone and wood. When Mary opened her store, so many customers wanted to stay over that she converted it into an inn. At Burgundy House almost everything is for sale, but guests have the opportunity to live for a day or so in the special atmosphere Mary Keenan has created.

The inn is furnished with a profusion of French country antiques, but when British conductor Neville Marriner stayed here, he said it reminded him of a snug little English inn. Perhaps Burgundy House is just the kind of place that makes everyone feel at home. There is always a fire going in the long, narrow common room in winter, and in summer everyone sits out on a secluded patio in the back and enjoys

79

**"Simple,
mais
convenable"**
and somewhat more; the
warm, unpretentious stone
front of Burgundy House
conceals a rich variety of
antiques. The inn's sign
features a vignette of
Napoleon III, an indication
of Burgundy House's
French bias.

Landscape
of the
grape.
The Napa Valley
vineyards, visible through
the window of the
common room.

the view over the vineyards to Mount Veeder, the highest point in this part of the valley.

The bedrooms are bright and cheerful, with flower paintings hung against the stone walls. The beds are of antique brass, iron or wood, worked with Victorian elaborateness. One has a luxurious fur throw and the others are covered with ruffled and richly patterned comforters. There is always a good local Napa Valley wine decanted in the bedrooms, and Mary maintains a selection of sherry, Burgundy and zinfandel in the common room.

The inn has grown since Mary and Bob opened it. Across the street are a splendidly spacious suite remodeled from a store that was once Yountville's justice court and a tiny house Mary has decorated in rich browns and deep reds.

Burgundy House is filled with personal touches. There is a chess set in the lobby, and a number of antique games. The sheets on the beds have the sheen and feel of silk, because Mary feels that people enjoy real luxury even in the most rustic country inn. She also feels that guests shouldn't have to worry about time, so there are no clocks anywhere.

Colorful
cupboard.
The festive quality of the
design is something one
notes in almost all of the
decorative accessories at
the inn. This cupboard was
painted by Dawn Devine, a
San Francisco artist.

The native influence.

Despite the prevalence of French furniture, many of the beds at Burgundy House are American, including this marvelous Victorian design, at left, made from gumwood, walnut and pine. A Chinese vase, above, sits in a classical, decorative niche. On the table is needlework Mary brought back from a visit to Hong Kong; an Italian lamp hangs above.

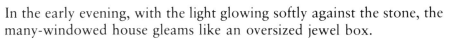

In the early evening, with the light glowing softly against the stone, the many-windowed house gleams like an oversized jewel box.

Burgundy House serves an unusually elaborate Continental breakfast: juice, fresh strawberries in hollowed-out pineapples, stewed rhubarb in clear glass dishes and a rich variety of pastries on silver platters. For lunch and dinner, there are several fine restaurants nearby. As interest in Napa Valley wines has grown, so has the list of local restaurants serving meals worthy of the best vintages.

A spirit of festivity seems to rest on Yountville. The town has a unique shopping center—Vintage 1870—just down the street from Burgundy House in the vast, remodeled Groezinger Winery. People can take champagne flights in a hot-air balloon that goes up from a nearby field, and the Keenans keep a British taxi to ferry guests from winery to winery. Talk at the inn is often of wine and food, but whatever is spoken of, the conversations have an unmistakable air of congeniality. Burgundy House and the Keenans somehow inspire this, and the happy result is that all their guests, from all over the world, feel extremely welcome there.

Tub for two.

With its oversized tub, antique shaving mirror and park bench appropriately placed to allow for conversations with bathers, the upstairs bathroom, shown here in two views, is a perfect place to enjoy a glass of local wine and pass the time of day.

CITY HOTEL

Columbia, California

Early in 1850 Dr. Thaddeus Hildreth and his brother George made camp in what was to become Columbia; they soon struck gold. The site was in the heart of the California Mother Lode, a mile-wide seam of gold-bearing quartz on the western ridge of the Sierra Nevadas, stretching 120 miles from Mariposa north to Georgetown. Within a month, some six thousand miners were working the area, and a canvas tent for selling whiskey and playing cards was soon put up, always a good sign that a mining town was growing. The area continued to prosper, and by 1852 it had more than 150 stores and saloons, along with a church, a Masonic Lodge and a Temperance League. The strike was a rich one—eventually miners would extract some $87 million in gold from the Columbia field—and the town felt the need for a little class in its public establishments. It found what it was looking for in 1856, when George Morgan built the "What Cheer House" on Main Street. When it burned down, along with most of the rest of the town, in 1867, George rebuilt it as Morgan's Hotel. Then, in 1874, he changed the name to City Hotel. In its time, the hotel has seen service as the office of the *Columbia Gazette,* the local opera house, an assay office and something called Cheap John Louis's Auction House.

It was as a combination hotel and tavern that the City Hotel was best known, and now, as a result of a massive renovation project undertaken by the State of California, it is once again in business. The City Hotel is the focal point of the Columbia State Historic Park. The entire community is now a working museum of the exciting Gold Rush days, including a little two-story 1860 schoolhouse; the Odd Fellows Hall, looking just as odd as it did in 1855; and a fire engine, Papeete,

Hardscrabble homestead.

This miner's cabin, left, and local jail, above, are reminders of a time when the hope of striking it rich induced thousands of men to leave civilized comforts behind. The jail was in use as late as 1930.

that was supposed to have been shipped to Tahiti by the Honneman Company in Boston but wound up in the California mountains.

As with most of the remaining buildings in Columbia, the City Hotel is built of brick. Its two-story facade features a set of French doors flanked by heavy iron shutters, which served the double purpose of fire control and protection from the boisterous miners who were not always careful about opening glass doors before going through them.

The public rooms are large by the standards of the day, but they do not, at first glance, seem to be particularly western. The prospectors who came to pan for gold in the Sierras had little interest in a new style of living. Many of them came from the East, and, as lonely men have a way of doing, they tried to recreate their old home in a new land. Brought overland by wagon, or by ship around Cape Horn, handsome, worthy pieces of solid, Victorian furniture would arrive at mining camps almost every day. Many came from Grand Rapids, made in the days when that Michigan city was synonymous with the best mass-produced furniture. The rooms at the City Hotel are a jumble of Victoriana that would have gladdened the heart of any homesick miner. A gorgeous rosewood piano, a nineteenth-century credenza with an oval mirror, several baroque Victorian sofas and rockers upholstered in tapestry are just a few of the treasures that brought a civilizing touch to a rough mining camp. The hotel's art collection covers the full range, from an enchantingly Victorian garland of flowers made from feathers framed under glass, to English engravings and Currier and Ives reproductions. One completely western piece of art hangs in the What

The hub

of Columbia's commercial district. The building below has housed a dry goods store since 1855. At right is the Wells Fargo office. *Overleaf,* the façade of the City Hotel today.

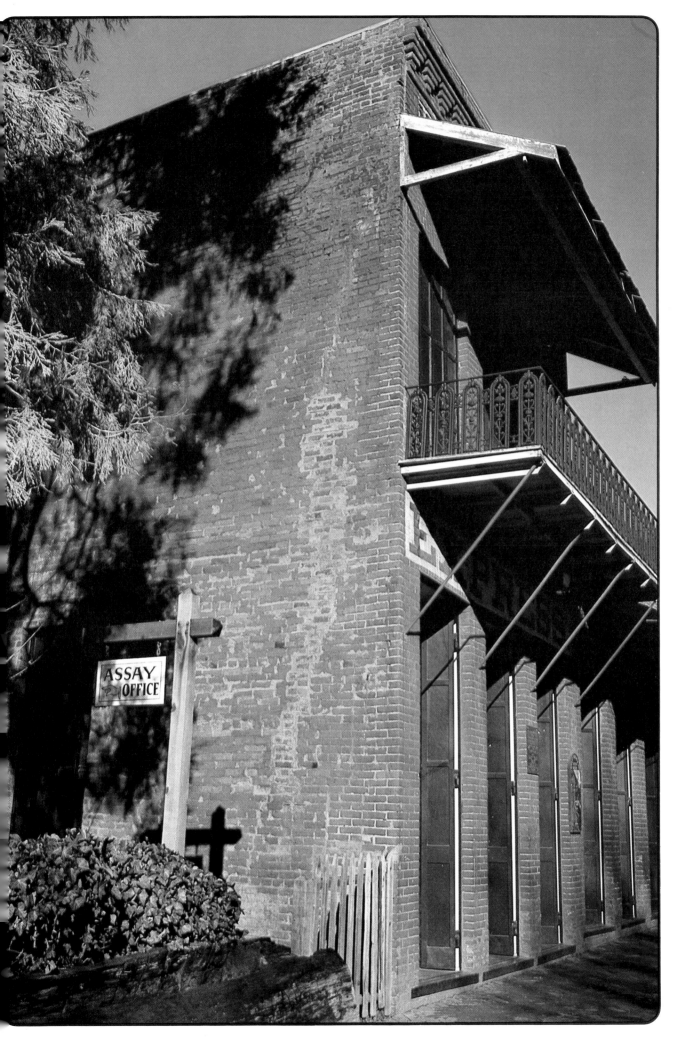

Heart
of gold.

Inside the simple brick building, the dining room, left, and saloon, above, display a surprisingly elaborate finish.

Cheer Saloon, an oil painting of Juanita, an excitable lady who stabbed a man to death and holds the distinction of being the only woman hanged in the Columbia goldfield.

The nine bedrooms are all decorated in appropriate Victorian style. Room 1, with its own door leading onto an upstairs balcony, is the star. The massive double bed, said to have once belonged to the warden at San Quentin Prison, is an elaborate affair of carved walnut. The dressing table is topped with Carrara marble. The rooms have half-baths, so guests must follow the nineteenth-century miner's custom of showering down the hall. Each guest is given a house robe and towel, and a small basket containing soap, washcloth and shower cap.

The biggest surprise at the City Hotel is the restaurant, which is happily not at all as it was in George Morgan's time. The chef is Barry Marcillac, who came to Columbia from Ernie's, one of San Francisco's finest restaurants. Under his direction, the City Hotel offers French cuisine served in the slightly florid restored dining room. Today's menus would have awed the hotel's first customers, who were accustomed to dining on beef jerky and cheap whiskey. Now, every dish is a production, and even something as simple as a lettuce and mushroom salad is served with each leaf of crisp, cold Kentucky limestone lettuce artistically arranged on the plate. The house specialties are roast quail and marinated hare, but Chef Marcillac produces a full range of dishes from a repertoire of international cuisine, including roast duck, château-briand and loin of lamb stuffed with spinach.

Camera ready.

The mirror of this Victorian vanity reflects one of the hotel's turn of the century beds. Columbia is so well preserved that it is often used for filming TV westerns.

The City Hotel is also an on-the-job training facility for students who are studying hotel and restaurant management at nearby Columbia Junior College. They often double as waiters and are particularly knowledgeable about the best vintages of fine California wines.

Three hours' drive from San Francisco, the City Hotel is an excellent starting place for investigating the wonders of Sierra country. After more than eighty years, the Sierra Railroad Company is still operating a few miles away in Jamestown, and the Mother Lode Cannonball makes the sixteen-mile run up to the highest of the old mining camps in an hour and a half.

The City Hotel is open year-round, but the principal season runs from April through October. Every summer, people come to these mountains, bringing with them a fascination for this exciting period in American history rather than a lust for gold. Thanks to a farsighted policy of California's Department of Parks and Recreation, and a healthy flow of tourist dollars, what might have been a ghost town is very much alive.

Sunstruck.

The inn's silver tea service rests on a desk in the living room.

SUTTER CREEK INN

Sutter Creek, California

Few men in American history have suffered a more ironic fate than John Sutter. An impoverished young man in Europe, Sutter left his wife and children behind him in Switzerland when he fled to America to escape his creditors. Determined to make his fortune on the western frontier, Sutter arrived in California in 1839, and less than ten years later he had built a vast personal empire and become one of the biggest land owners and cattle ranchers in the territory. Then, in 1848, James Marshall, a carpenter working at Sutter's sawmill in Coloma on the south fork of the American River, discovered flakes of gold in the river water. Soon hundreds of thousands of prospectors swarmed over Sutter's property, slaughtering his livestock and stealing his land. Three years later, while many of the Forty-Niners were becoming rich, Sutter was bankrupt. He spent the rest of his life in poverty, desperately seeking restitution for his lost properties.

Sutter Creek is fifty miles south of the initial strike, and its name commemorates the time Sutter camped here by the stream with a scouting party, just before his land was overrun—perhaps the last peaceful interlude the man was ever to know. Sutter Creek is a quiet town, and it is fascinating to stroll among its simple Gold Rush homes of red, yellow and blue painted wood, with their small, neatly tended gardens. The town grew up around the diggings that eventually became famous mines—the Eureka and Leland Stanford's Lincoln Mine among them.

Within the town of Sutter Creek is the tiny enclave that comprises the Sutter Creek Inn. Built in 1859 by one of the town's leading merchants for his New Hampshire bride, and later owned by a state senator, the inn started out as a Greek Revival cottage. But the addition of a long

Fire thorn.

Pyracanth berries flame outside the white calm of Sutter Creek's Victorian bay window.

Welcoming spaces.

Comfort and conversation are staples at Sutter Creek. Guests assemble at nine in the morning at the two long tables in the inn's breakfast room, above left, and after breakfast they often retire to the living room, bottom left. A sled-topped coffee table sits between the two couches.

ell and a porch gave it its own distinctive flair. It is a typical American home that grew and expanded to serve the needs of successive generations.

The old place had been unlived in for several years when Jane Way discovered it, in 1966, while driving through the Gold Rush country with her children. Jane fell in love with it, and after extended negotiations with the absentee owner, she bought it and converted it into the Sutter Creek Inn.

The inn is a comfortable, happy place, filled with Jane's family's furniture and the results of her acquisitive visits to antiques stores throughout the country. The living room affords relaxation in any one of several upholstered chairs and sofas. There is a spinet piano and an unusual low table made from an old toboggan. The most splendid pieces in the room are a large chest from Quebec, and a beautiful, big hutch with a spoon rack, from Boston. These two country pieces set the tone for the inn: ample proportions with exquisite, fine lines, and readiness to stand up to the requirements of daily use.

In the rear of the main house is the huge, eat-in kitchen, where Jane serves her well-known family breakfasts to overnight guests at nine o'clock sharp. Jane thwacks a big gong, announcing breakfast, and it's up to the guests to get to the table, because she isn't going to wait around for them. No one needs to be coaxed. The kitchen is a cheerful, brick and wood-paneled room, hung with copper utensils. Guests sit at two long pine tables, while Jane and her staff cook up a giant

breakfast, with platters of eggs, sometimes fixed Mexican-style, stacks of pancakes, homemade muffins and great bowls of fresh fruit salad. The fresh coffee is liberally laced with brandy, for those who wish it. At one time, Jane waited up for her guests to have a nightcap with them, but they kept coming in later and later. "They were all out having fun, and I thought, unless I can do the same—which I can't, because someone has to watch the inn—I'm going to bed," says Jane. Now she serves the brandy in the morning. Jane serves no other meals, but she posts a list of the eating places in the area, with her own capsule restaurant reviews.

Jane is both the owner and the social director of the Sutter Creek Inn. A knowledgeable historian of the surrounding area, she is an excellent source of information on the various sights in this Gold Rush country. She also can be persuaded to give palm readings in the afternoon, privately, in the living room.

Jane had originally intended just to use the main house for the inn, but she has expanded by converting the old service buildings in the back into guest accommodations. These small structures have all kept the names of their original functions: the Miner's Cabin, the Upper Washhouse, the Cellar Room and the Woodshed. The grounds around the buildings are landscaped with walkways, little gardens and shade trees, so that in spring and summer they turn into a peaceful retreat.

Each little house is different. Some have luxurious sunken bathtubs and their own fireplaces. Jane has decorated each to her own wide-ranging taste. A room could combine Parisian-print wallpaper from the 1950s with splashes of vibrant, modern colors, French Provincial chairs, cream-colored canopy beds and a wood-burning stove that might have graced a miner's cabin in the back country.

The Sutter Creek Inn is known also for its "swinging" beds, which are suspended from the ceiling by chains. Jane came across the idea when visiting a friend who had rigged one up as a compromise between a hammock and a regular bed. They can be anchored in a stationary position, but adventurous guests find they can accustom themselves to the gentle rocking in fairly short order.

"Once you get used to them," Jane points out, "they're much more comfortable than water beds. I'd give it about two nights."

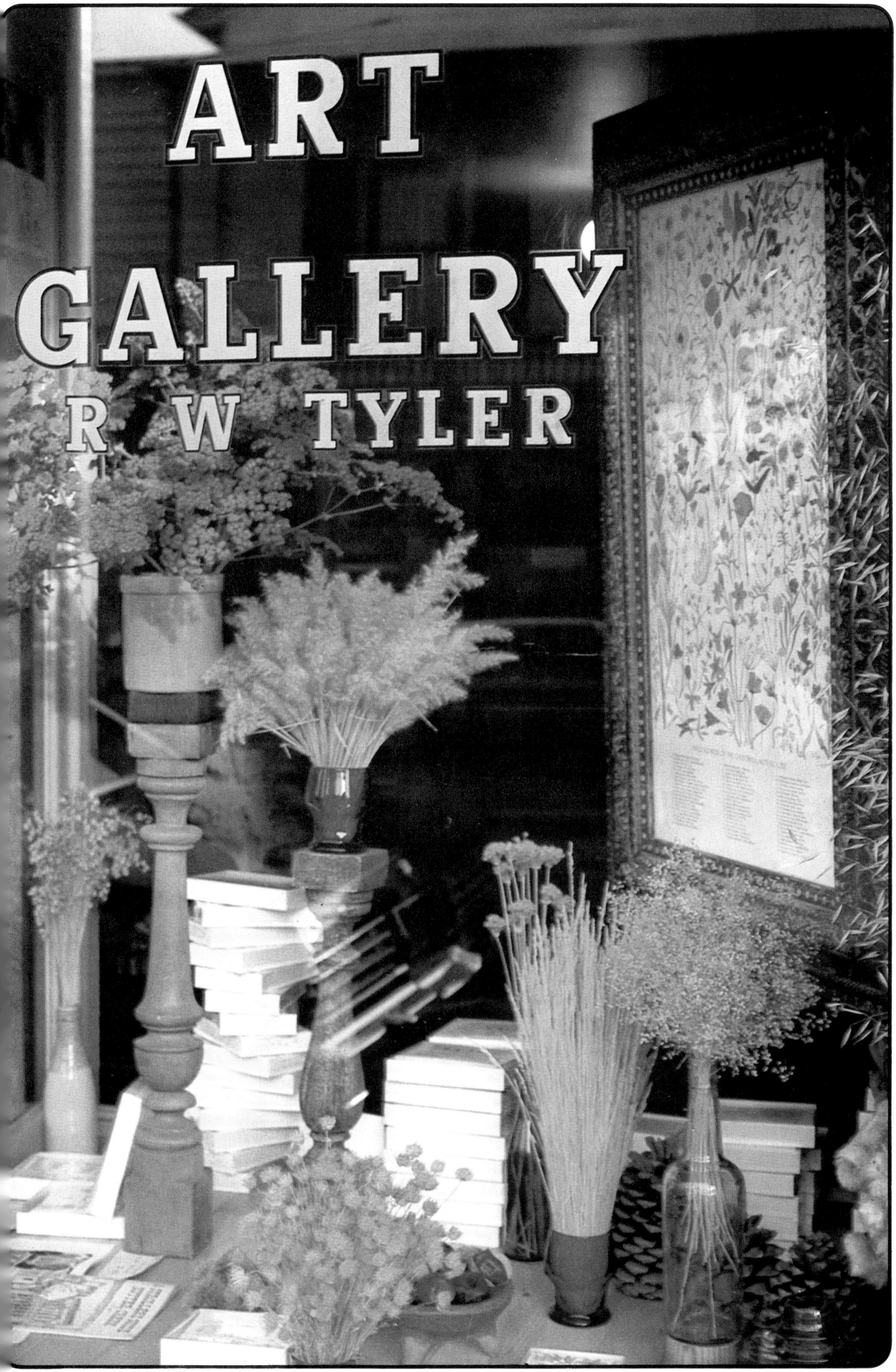
ART
GALLERY
R W TYLER

Poet's place.

Carmel, with its wide beach and cypress-fringed shoreline, began as an artists' colony but has grown into a resort community.

VAGABOND HOUSE

Carmel-by-the-Sea, California

Outdoor living room.

Two California live oaks provide shade for the courtyard at Vagabond House. The proliferation of plants includes gigantic staghorn ferns, tree fuchsias, camellia bushes and cyclamens. One of the inn's two carousel horses, inset, is a splendid two-seater.

"There is always something different in bloom here in our garden," says Patsy Watts, as she sits in the shade of a pair of California live oak trees on the patio of Vagabond House. "And the permanent evergreens make an ideal background for the seasonal changes."

In the spring there are primroses, Japanese magnolias and daffodils. In the summer roses flourish, along with fuchsias and hydrangeas. The camellias come out in the fall, and during the winter the garden is splashed with the deep red of poinsettias. Only a few blocks away are the shops, art galleries and restaurants that have made Carmel internationally famous. Within easy reach by car are the redwoods at Big Sur, the trails through the rugged Santa Lucia Mountains and the oceanside vistas of Point Lobos State Reserve, which has been called "the greatest meeting of land and water in the world."

Vagabond House started out simply enough. It was built in 1941 as a series of efficiency apartments during the World War II building boom. But with love and care for detail, they have become a country inn of immeasurable grace and charm.

From the outside, Vagabond House presents itself as a group of neat white stucco cottages built into the side of a gently rising hill. A curving path leads up into the garden courtyard in the center of the complex. The charm of the place is due to the efforts of Chuck and Patsy Watts, who have owned the inn since 1974 and have filled it with the fruits of a lifetime of collecting. On a shelf of the reception room is an elegant mantel clock that once belonged to the University Club in Los Angeles. It is just one of twenty-three clocks from Chuck's collection that have been placed around the house. Patsy's contributions are an almost incalculable number of teddy bears—she loves them—and superb

102

Extravaganza time.

Patsy's needlepoint decorates both the cushions of the couch and the wall, where examples are framed among a potpourri of drawings and paintings. Her teddy bear collection and Chuck's clock collection are both in evidence. Chuck got the unusual oak chair in Washington State and likes it because he feels "it's one of a kind," a quality the Wattses value in every object that goes into the inn. The distinguished-looking dog pictured on the needlepoint cushion is Muffin, the Wattses' Afghan.

Vagabond loot.

The old, fine, curious and fresh are combined in the decoration of rooms at Vagabond House, left and above right, and in the shops of Carmel, above, where looking can be raised to the status of an art.

examples of her own needlework, done as pillows or framed as pictures in the rooms.

Most of the Wattses' guests come to settle in; they stay for a week, a month or even a whole season. Most of the rooms are large enough to be bedroom and sitting room as well. Several have fireplaces, and since the complex was originally apartments, many of the rooms have their own kitchens.

The Wattses have an eclectic and whimsical sense of decoration. Room 10 has a mirror with an Oriental-looking carved wood frame, pine-paneled walls and an eighteenth-century country desk. In one corner a modern oil painting of Vagabond House is set on a Victorian easel. Room 3 is done in a nautical motif, with brass seafaring instruments and a ship's model on the mantel, but it also has an English white oak secretary and a stunning needlework re-creation of a Picasso painting. "I *like* themes," says Patsy. "I'm not so enthusiastic about them," Chuck admits. Room 8 features an odd lawn bowls trophy whose wooden globes open up into humidor compartments; in the window sits a black cast-iron horse from a babies' carousel. All the rooms are unusually well stocked with books. Chuck and Patsy happened on a cache of 1930s hardcover mysteries, still in their original jackets, and these are shelved in the rooms along with recent novels and nonfiction, old anthologies of "best-loved works" and *National Geographic* back issues. Every room either opens directly onto the garden or overlooks it.

Service at Vagabond House is informal but extremely gracious and attentive. Patsy puts fresh flowers in the rooms almost every day. In the mornings, guests open their door to the morning's *San Francisco Chronicle* on the doorstep and walk through the garden to the reception room to pick up their Continental breakfast of fruit juice and sweet rolls from an old-fashioned tea cart. Eating in the patio is popular, but many guests take their breakfast back to their rooms on trays. The Wattses provide fresh-ground coffee and percolators in the rooms.

At Vagabond House even the squirrels are coddled. Several who make their home in the courtyard have such elevated tastes that they will not eat regular peanuts, so Chuck and Patsy feed them on a steady diet of the fresh-roasted variety.

UNION HOTEL
Los Alamos, California

The Union Hotel looks like an ordinary western hotel. The dining room is large and somewhat formal, dominated by a gigantic grandfather clock. The bar is a truly noble affair, hewn from solid African mahogany. The bedrooms upstairs are romantically attractive, with pedestal sinks, sleigh beds with handmade quilts and a decanter of Sebastiani wine on the dresser. But the Union Hotel is not any ordinary kind of hotel. It is an event. More specifically, it is the somewhat eccentric extension of its owner, Dick Langdon.

In 1972, Mr. Langdon, a highly successful meat wholesaler from Los Angeles, decided it was time to change his lifestyle. He considered buying some ranch property up north; instead, he wound up in the virtual ghost town of Los Alamos, buying an abandoned hotel that had been boarded up for nineteen years.

Deciding to restore this 1880 relic, he sallied forth on the first of a year-long series of antiquing trips to furnish his new establishment. Among the items he returned with are a pair of 200-year-old Egyptian burial urns, a handmade lamp that was used in the movie *Gone With the Wind,* the headlights from a 1914 Oldsmobile and a pair of swinging doors from a nineteenth-century New Orleans bordello.

Jim Radhe is responsible for the details of the restoration. He had done some paint contracting work for Dick early in 1972 and later was offered a job. Within a week, Jim arrived at the door with his luggage and has lived at the hotel ever since.

The first time guests come to the hotel, they are allowed to stay only one night, because Dick wants to make sure he likes his guests before letting them stay longer. They are, however, permitted to pick their

Western swing.

The furnishings at the Union Hotel are as eclectic as they are elaborate in recreating a "western hotel" interior. The dining room, left, admirably illustrates the hotel's atmosphere. The lamp on the sitting room desk, above, was used in *Gone with the Wind.* Set beneath flowered skylights, the tremendous pool table, *overleaf,* is in a central hall that links the upstairs bedrooms in a typically western fashion.

own rooms. They just go upstairs, find a room they like, tell the clerk which one they've selected and he'll give them a key.

There is no menu at the Union Hotel; guests eat whatever the management is serving that night. The meal always starts with cheese and crackers and a homemade soup. The most popular is Leather Apron soup, a hearty combination of chicken and noodles cooked the way it used to be on the old wagon trails. This is usually followed by a beef or chicken dish and silky-smooth cornbread. When Dick thinks his patrons should know the details about what they're having that night, he'll let them know. Dinner is prix fixe for adults; children pay by weight—their own. When youngsters come to the hotel, Dick slings them on a huge butcher's scale, and the heavier they are, the more their parents pay for their dinner. The Continental breakfast served to the overnight guests includes gingerbread cake, chocolate chip cookies, pound cake and a bottle of brandy.

After dinner, as often as not, the entertainment comes from Dick's private collection of old radio suspense programs, such as "The Shadow" and "The Green Hornet."

The Union Hotel is not an ordinary hotel. It is open all year, but only on Fridays, Saturdays and Sundays. "Three days a week is fun," Dick explains. "Beyond that, it becomes work."

A shot in the dark.

At the Union Hotel, guests find themselves either luxuriating in the pattern-filled spaces of the upstairs rooms or downing a shot of whiskey in the traditional western bar on the right.

SAN YSIDRO RANCH

Montecito, California

Getting away.

San Ysidro Ranch has been attracting celebrities for years to its magnificent spread of ocean front woodlands. Not all guests are well-known, but each gets VIP treatment. At left is the oldest building on the property, an 1825 adobe cottage that has been preserved as a museum. The inn's accommodations are cottages placed around the grounds, like the one above.

"How beautiful when the wood smoke goes up straight, and the pepper trees stand unstirring, and behind the screen of tall eucalyptus trees the fallen sun glows, a long slow fire over the sea, and the lavender-colour mist rises between. How beautiful, the mountains behind us, remote in that late light, a little unearthly.

"The loveliness of these evenings moves the heart. . . . There is something in it all of that dream, as of Paradise, which stirred the Italian painters in the old days. Well may it be sainted—San Ysidro."

So wrote John Galsworthy, when he was staying at the San Ysidro Ranch, working on the final revisions of *The Forsyte Saga,* during the early glory days of the ranch. And what days they were! One of the oldest guest accommodations in California, San Ysidro Ranch was a premier resort almost from the day it opened in 1893. Situated in the foothills above Montecito near Santa Barbara, this great ranch that had once been used as a way station for Franciscan monks attracted famous guests from all over the world. It was a particular favorite of well-known writers who came to find solitude in one of the ranch's thirty-nine cottages. Sinclair Lewis favored the Eucalyptus Cottage, and Somerset Maugham retired to the flower-bordered Geranium Cottage to write his short stories. Winston Churchill came here to work on the manuscript of one of his prose works and noted, "It is difficult to imagine a more delightful situation."

For some thirty years, until his death in 1958, San Ysidro Ranch was owned by screen star Ronald Colman, who ran it as an exclusive hideaway for his friends and celebrated guests. Such stars as Bing Crosby and Jack Benny would retreat to the ranch cottages to get away from the Hollywood grind, and Vivien Leigh and Laurence Olivier

dashed here to marry. In 1953, John F. Kennedy, then the junior senator from Massachusetts, honeymooned here with his wife.

Visiting the ranch today, it is easy to see why it has been such a famous resort for so long. Its 540 acres of wooded hillside contain some of the most breathtaking scenery in the state. At San Ysidro Ranch, even the tennis courts have views of the Pacific Ocean on one side and the Santa Ynez Mountains on the other. The accommodations are so extensive, some guests bring their own horses.

Incredibly, for all its peerless reputation, San Ysidro Ranch was almost lost. It was saved at the last minute by the dream of a pair of hard-working, transplanted New Yorkers—and a great deal of money.

After Colman's death, the resort had a number of owners, and it grew seedier with each change. By 1976, the once-proud ranch was a dilapidated horror, with cottages in disrepair and bridle trails choked with overgrowth. In stepped Jim Lavenson, the former president of the Plaza Hotel in New York, and his wife, Suzie. Jim was actually looking for a small hotel to buy in Santa Barbara, but the challenge of reviving the proud heritage of San Ysidro Ranch was too compelling. He bought the place for $800,000 and promptly put another $500,000 into refurbishing the complex.

"It was really in terrible shape," Jim recalls. "For all the houses, the maintenance crew consisted of one gardener, one lawn mower and a vacuum cleaner that didn't work."

Jim and Suzie poured their money into the place and put in eighteen

The public face

of the very private inn is the dining room. Its simple walls and elaborate mirror create a subdued and intimate setting for dinner. The inn's symbol adorns the doorway of inlaid wood, which opens into the Plow and Angel Bar.

Private place.

The back deck of the Forest Cottage, below, is so secluded that the outside world might seem to have completely disappeared.

hours a day of their own time. Now there is a staff of ninety-six at the ranch, including five gardeners and four maintenance people. San Ysidro Ranch has come back, and, if possible, it is better than ever.

San Ysidro is named after Saint Isadore, the patron saint of Madrid. According to legend, Isadore, a Spanish shepherd, was such a kind and benevolent man that the Lord sent down a guardian angel to tend his flock while Isadore tended to the sick and the needy. Today, San Ysidro Ranch, according to Jim, "benevolently tends to the well and the not so needy."

The ranch is a lush resort facility with private bungalow accommodations dedicated to giving its guests the ultimate in personal service. Upon arrival at the main house, guests are introduced to their bellman, who drives them to their cottage in a golf cart. By the time they get there, their name will already have been posted on a wooden sign outside their bungalow, and it will stay there as long as they are guests. The symbolism is clear: as long as they are at San Ysidro Ranch, they are at home. Jim feels that most of his guests come for the privacy afforded by the individual cottages, nestled in seclusion amid the artful landscaping.

Each cottage is completely different in size and decoration from the other. Suzie has undertaken the gigantic decoration task by emptying their own New York home of all its furnishings, as well as by buying from the Salvation Army, ordering from J. C. Penney and finding priceless antiques. The most popular and expensive accommodation is the Forest Cottage. It is a former ranch hand's bungalow that has been

115

completely modernized, with a brand-new kitchen, superb modern and period furniture, and that new California necessity for the good life, a private whirlpool bath enclosed behind a redwood fence.

Guests need never appear outside their own cottages if they don't want to, and many of them don't. For those who do want to socialize, there is the Hacienda Lounge. There, from eleven every morning, the management runs an "honor bar," where guests make their own drinks and keep track of their tab.

San Ysidro Ranch has recaptured the exciting ambiance of the 1930s and 1940s, when it was Ronald Colman's mountain snuggery. It also effectively recalls its even earlier history, when it was part of a series of Franciscan mission houses along the coast of California. One old adobe cottage, which dates back to 1826, is still standing. The ranch's working bar was built in 1850 as part of the wine cellar, and customers now dine formally in what once was the mission's citrus fruit-packing house. The resort's restaurant is one of the most discriminating in the state. The chef, Camille Schwartz, a native of Lorraine in France, supervises a kitchen that serves both traditional western fare and the most exotic delights of haute cuisine with equal ease. Many Californians prefer the thick grilled steaks and tender prime ribs; however, such dishes as fresh artichoke hearts with prawns in mustard sauce and sautéed Wisconsin veal with Dubonnet are what keep bringing back television's French chef, Julia Child, who always goes to the kitchen afterward for a chat with Camille.

Although Jim and Suzie have already put a tremendous amount of time and effort into their ranch, much remains to be done. There are several rooms and cottages Suzie wants to refurbish when she finds the time and money to do so. The maintenance of so many old buildings is fearsome. Occasionally, a radiator will go bang in the night or a lightbulb will dim out, but the setting at San Ysidro Ranch is so rapturous that no one seems to mind.

"The people who come here," says Suzie, "want to return to a tradition, and if that means a leaky faucet, they don't mind. They're not hung up on little things like that. Our guests aren't looking for status. They already have that."

THE INN
AT RANCHO SANTA FE

Rancho Santa Fe, California

One of the best mistakes

a railroad ever made was planting this grove of eucalyptus. The Inn at Rancho Santa Fe now sits on more than twenty acres of the planting, a lush tropical garden where bougainvillea, acacia, magnolia, palm trees, wild flowers and even strawberries flourish. Above, the tiled roof of one of the inn's cottages.

The forty-foot-high eucalyptus trees that give the Inn at Rancho Santa Fe its luxuriant, junglelike setting were all part of a dreadful mistake. In 1906, the Atcheson, Topeka and Santa Fe Railroad purchased almost nine thousand acres of unpromising Southern California countryside that had once been part of a Mexican land grant. The idea was that the company, hoping to ensure itself of a permanent supply of wooden railroad ties for its expanding operations, would literally grow its own. The Santa Fe planted three million seedlings imported from Australia in the sandy California soil, and the exotic trees shot up like weeds. Unfortunately, when the railroad later discovered that is was impossible to cut a flat, usable tie out of the twisted trunk of a eucalyptus tree, the project had to be abandoned. The trees continued to flourish, and the railroad decided to turn the rest of the unplanted acreage into a citrus farm, with a part set aside for residential development.

The first structure, built of adobe blocks in the traditional California mission style, was used to accommodate prospective land buyers and is now the main building of the inn. In 1941, George Richardson bought the building and some surrounding acreage with an eye toward turning it into a quiet resort where guests could enjoy a bit of peace in the California sun. Over the years, he added more cottages, gardens and walkways until the Inn at Rancho Santa Fe became a tiny little community all its own, where some seventy-five guests could enjoy the more than twenty acres of lush surroundings in leisurely seclusion. It was the perfect place for Mary Pickford to come to get away from the clamor of Hollywood. The eminent judge Harold Medina once spent

High, wide and then some.

There is a basic grandness to the interior design. Left, the main lounge sports the family's collection of antique sailing ships and their grandmother's treasures from the Orient. Above, the breakfast room overlooks the swimming pool.

a month here, relaxing in one of the cottages while translating a book into Greek.

In 1958, the inn was sold to Stephen W. Royce, a well-known California hotelier, and has remained in the Royce family ever since.

The Inn at Rancho Santa Fe remains a quiet complex of small cottages set amidst a flourish of vibrant, almost tropical, greenery. A Brazilian pepper plant twines around the front door of the main building, and out on the grounds are stands of eucalyptus, acacia, avocado and palm trees interlaced with the purple of bougainvillea blossoms. The acreage requires five grounds keepers working full-time to tend the gardens, which are filled with ornamental flowers and terraces of rose bushes.

The cottages are simply and comfortably outfitted with western-style furniture. Most of them have their own secluded porches. The emphasis at the inn is on ease and comfort rather than on dramatic architectural or design effects.

It is a home of quiet pleasures. There is tennis on the property, and golfing arrangements can be made on any of three nearby courses. The inn maintains its own beach cottage at Del Mar for its guests and will readily pack them a picnic lunch.

The town of Rancho Santa Fe is a small, prosperous community that strives for homogeneity—a board of architects supervises all construction in the area. All the shops and buildings are cast in the same Spanish-style mold as the inn.

The inn's main building serves as both a clubhouse for guests and

A natural order.

There are twenty separate cottages on the grounds, many named for flowers or trees. Above left is Honeysuckle. Private patios such as the one at right are attached to many of the cottages. Five full-time grounds keepers are on hand to care for the landscaping.

one of the principal social centers for the community. There are four dining areas, including the charming book-lined Library Room, and the Patio Room, which in the summer opens out onto a patio flanked with brilliant poinsettias and hanging plants.

The lounge area, a favorite place both before and after dinner, is one of the most spectacular rooms likely to be found in a western country inn. A huge, thirty-by-forty-foot room, it is filled with Royce family heirlooms. Mr. Royce's grandmother had traveled in China and returned with some exquisite examples of Oriental arts and crafts. Wall tapestries, dolls, countless vases and bowls, and a magnificent piece of needlework done in gold thread are some of the treasures on display.

In this age of computerized hotel keeping, the Inn at Rancho Santa Fe insists on maintaining the old traditions. Dan Royce, the present innkeeper, requires the staff to know the guests' names *before* they arrive. Dan appears willing to give a guest the shirt off his back, and if not that, at least his jacket. One evening a guest appeared for dinner without the requisite coat, and Dan loaned him his. Naturally, it fit.

Heavy timbers

form the *vigas*, or beams, of the sitting room, where magnificent artifacts of the Spanish colonial period are displayed. Though the buildings themselves are modern, the building methods are traditional.

RANCHO ENCANTADO

Tesuque, New Mexico

Almost one hundred years before the Pilgrims landed at Plymouth Rock, men from Europe had come to this part of the country seeking fortune and adventure. Francisco Vásquez de Coronado arrived first in 1540 to search for the legendary seven cities of gold but found only Indian pueblo villages. By 1581, the first major roadway in the New World was serving travelers from Chihuahua, Mexico, to what would become Santa Fe, New Mexico.

At first glance, Rancho Encantado today would seem to be a relic of those ancient times. Only eight miles from modern Sante Fe, Rancho Encantado is a secluded complex in the chaparral country of New Mexico. Its heavily beamed roofs and spanking white adobe walls would have been the pride of any sixteenth-century conquistador. Actually, Rancho Encantado is a modern, highly sophisticated hotel operation that in only the last ten years has become one of the premier resort facilities in America while still retaining the atmosphere and amenities of an old southwestern ranch.

The original main structure was built around 1920—no one is absolutely certain exactly when—and until 1967 the ranch was a small country hotel with twelve rooms and two cottages. It was then that the energetic Betty Egan bought the place and set about transforming it. She expanded the main building and added more cottages. Each accommodation at Rancho Encantado is scrupulously faithful to the traditional adobe ranch style. Made of adobe, brick and hand-painted tile, the rooms are decorated with authentic Indian rugs, wall hangings and art objects from the area. Most of the rooms have their own patios where guests can sit out and see the magnificent horizon of the Sangre de Cristo and Jemez mountains in the distance. Mrs. Egan has added

Adobe pillars

uphold the arch over a gate at Rancho Encantado, a perfect place for chilies to dry in the full sun of a New Mexico day.

Rich relations

between the heavy Spanish colonial decoration and the simple materials of the building are evident in these pictures: the split-level dining room, left; the brick-floored patio, above; the tiled corner, right; and the bedroom, far right, whose beams retain their natural circular shape.

tennis courts, a swimming pool, a stable and corral for the rancho's own herd of trained horses and a kitchen that has brought Rancho Encantado the reputation of being one the finest restaurants in the state. Guests have their choice of traditional southwestern dishes such as *huevos rancheros* and *chiles rellenos* along with the finest of traditional international cuisine. Surprisingly, Rancho Encantado is especially famous for its seafood, which is flown in fresh from the Pacific coast every day.

"We call ourselves a guest ranch rather than a dude ranch," Mrs. Egan explains. By whatever label, Rancho Encantado with its comfortable elegance and conscientious service has developed a loyal clientele who usually have to make reservations far in advance for its sixty accommodations. Some come for the riding and the summer sports. Some prefer to go sightseeing along the same trails first made by men who were here more than four hundred years ago searching for "gold, glory and God." Others just enjoy the food and relax in the warm New Mexico sunshine.

Rancho Encantado has become a particular favorite of world-famous celebrities such as Prince Rainier and Princess Grace of Monaco and Nelson Rockefeller, who arrive knowing that their privacy will be respected by the other guests. If first-time visitors get the feeling they have seen Rancho Encantado before, it's because they probably have. The rancho and the surrounding countryside have long been a choice location for filming motion pictures, and the ranch has served as a home base for such stars as Henry Fonda, Jimmy Stewart, John Wayne and Gregory Peck, who have stayed there while on location.

Like all personally run operations, Rancho Encantado is an extension of its innkeeper. As Betty Egan says: "We are not a hotel in the usual sense; each room is furnished differently. We keep everything on a personal level. I get to know each of our guests—and our guests all get to know each other. There is a spirit of hospitality in the Southwest that's summed up in the expression, '*Mi casa, su casa,*' which means, 'My house is your house.' That's the way we feel here."

Chaparral country.

Overleaf: the Rancho Encantado makes a perfect journey's end in this rugged but beautiful New Mexico countryside.

ARIZONA INN

Tuscon, Arizona

It is appropriate that a place as gracious as the Arizona Inn should have come about as the result of an act of compassion by a kind lady. Isabella Greenway came from a family prominent in eastern society and was a bridesmaid at the wedding of Franklin and Eleanor Roosevelt. Later moving to Arizona, she became a noted rancher, artist and the only congresswoman in the history of the state. In 1927, she founded a handicraft shop to create jobs for unemployed World War I veterans, who were put to work making western-style furniture. Unfortunately, the Great Depression of 1929 knocked the bottom out of the business. Mrs. Greenway, not having the heart to tell her ex-soldiers to stop, created this spacious country resort to have a place for the furniture they were making.

Adding a mixture of her own family heirlooms and antiques along with some fine examples of contemporary Mexican-American crafts, Mrs. Greenway opened the inn in 1930 as a hideaway for her wealthy friends. For many years the John D. Rockefeller family wintered here, and the inn's swimming pool was largely added so that young Nelson and David would have a place to splash about in. Winston Churchill, Salvador Dali, Cary Grant and the Duke and Duchess of Windsor were all once guests at the inn.

Although the resort is considerably more relaxed under the present ownership of Mrs. Greenway's son John, there is still an air of Old World gentility about the Arizona Inn. The registration card has a place for the name of the guest's chauffeur. General manager Robert Minerich supervises an unusually large staff who take care of the eighty-six cottage rooms. Included in the staff is a full-time interior designer who is on hand to ensure that the décor is always up to standard.

131

Desert oasis.

Decorated in the soft beige, gray and clay-red tones of the desert, the bar, left, and main lounge, above, are an interior reflection of the surrounding landscape.

Simplicity and grandeur.

Amidst the fourteen acres of well-irrigated Arizona desert, guests can find privacy in any one of the 86 cottage rooms. The congenially large space of the library, right, is carpeted with soft, lush Moroccan rugs.

There are twenty gardeners, and, because of the exceptionally dry Tucson climate, the grass has to be reseeded twice a year to keep it the proper shade of green.

The cottage rooms range from single accommodations, furnished in a straightforward modern style, to the expansive two-bedroom house with its own servants' quarters and dining facilities that was used by the Rockefeller family.

The inn is made of a soft, coral adobe highlighted by shutters and trim of a brisk Williamsburg blue. The rooms are baronial affairs made charmingly intimate by light western touches. The library is big, comfortable and high-ceilinged, broken up into several separate sitting areas, including two long white couches in front of the huge fireplace.

The bar is a visual delight. Open and sunny, it is a study in soft beige and gray, accented by a huge, central skylight that lets the sun stream in on the ten-foot-high palm tree that serves as the room's focal point.

The dining room is spacious, painted white and is set off by cheerful, bright green tablecloths. Twenty-year-old John Stricker is the remark-

Overleaf, a rear view of the low-lying inn.

Framed spaces.

The dining room, right, is pleasant, high and open. The Arizona Inn offers guests the kind of individual attention that has long since been impossible at the larger resorts. A finger bowl, above, follows the meal. Paths and arbors articulate a desert landscape well tended, well watered and restrained.

ably young chef in charge, who has already acquired such a high reputation that many people make the two-hour drive from Phoenix just to come for dinner. The menu is Continental, with a few individual flourishes such as the Arizona Inn Special: eggplant sautéed with medallions of tenderloin and artichoke hearts.

When the Arizona Inn first opened, it was deep in the desert. But Tucson's building boom finally caught up with the inn, and it now is part of the suburban scene. It even has a numbered street address where before there wasn't even a street.

The Arizona Inn continues to fend off both urbanization and modernization. At a time when hotels are supposed to reach for the sky while sitting on the least possible amount of land, the inn spreads itself out over fourteen acres. When more and more restaurants are relying on precooked, preprocessed and frozen foods, the kitchen at the inn still prepares everything from scratch.

"The giants of the industry say that a place like this can't exist," says Robert Minerich. "Well, we're out to prove them wrong."

TANQUE VERDE RANCH

Tucson, Arizona

Ridin' high.

Nestled in the mountains above Tucson at an altitude of nearly three thousand feet, Tanque Verde Ranch is surrounded by expansive and breathtaking desert riding trails. A few of the inn's 85 horses, above, get a respite. For nonriders and those a bit sore from the previous day's outing, the front porch, *overleaf,* combines typical Spanish ranch architecture with thick-cushioned chairs.

The dude ranch is an extraordinary phenomenon that could only have developed in America. Nobody is exactly sure who was responsible for the idea, but most of the credit usually goes to author Owen Wister. Born in Pennsylvania and educated at Harvard, Wister spent several summers in Wyoming for his health and fell in love with the western frontier. His stories and books, particularly his most famous novel, *The Virginian*, published in 1903, fascinated armchair travelers in the East. Before long, tenderfoots were flocking to ranches in the West and were actually paying money to work as cowboys so they could experience firsthand the kind of life that Wister had so effectively described.

Tanque Verde Ranch, founded by Rafael Carillo on a Spanish land grant in 1862, is one of the oldest ranches in America now being used as a guest facility.

The ranch is one of the most luxurious of country inns, featuring indoor and outdoor swimming pools, whirlpool baths, air-conditioned rooms and a dining room whose chef likes to whip up such desserts as

Range roving.

Riding is almost a full-time activity at Tanque Verde; day trips are often planned around that greatest of all incentives, a midride meal.

**Children
are welcome**

at the ranch, which has
two counselors on staff to
attend to the needs of pint-
size cowboys.

143

mocha marzipan torte. But the lifestyle here vividly recalls the days when, for nearly one hundred years, Tanque Verde was one of the best ranches in Arizona.

The emphasis is on riding, so much so that unlimited horseback riding is included in the room rate. The ranch has more than eighty horses, and three full-time wranglers. Most of the social program of the ranch revolves around trail riding. In the morning, for example, guests may ride to breakfast at the old, abandoned hut up the road and then take to the trails for the second ride of the day. Usually led by head wrangler Mel Becker, the image of a western cowboy, the trail ride may wind around the countryside, across meandering streams and up the pebbly mountains, until the company winds up at Grand View, with its incredible vistas of the mountains beyond. If trail riding isn't enough, there's a weekly rodeo for the guests, where everyone gets at least one blue ribbon just for showing up. The few who don't want to ride that day can spend their time rallying on the ranch's private tennis

Out in the open.

Tanque Verde sits in the midst of over 1,500,000 acres in one of the world's few remaining untarnished wildernesses. Saguaro cactus, above, grows throughout the land around the ranch. The stonework around the pool adds drama to an already spectacular landscape.

courts; playing golf at one of the six championship courses nearby; or just snoozing in a hammock, waiting for the next barbecue. Tanque Verde is also a bird-watcher's paradise. Bob Cote is a particularly avid "birder" and organizes weekly bird-banding expeditions. Bob will band as many as fifty different species in a given year. Birds are everywhere: they sing the guests to sleep at night and wake them in the morning.

The bedrooms and suites are all ranch-style, with low beamed ceilings and brick walls. Most of the rooms have their own adobe fireplaces and all lead out onto their own private lounging area. The main building, which was built in the early 1870s, is a solid, L-shaped ranch house with walls almost two feet thick. While the building is the spacious, graceful kind that one would expect of an elegant inn, there are reminders of the earlier days when life on the range was not always a vacation. The few windows on the valley side of the ranch are quite small and were once used as gun ports for protection against marauding Indians.

One of the most popular spots at the Tanque Verde Ranch is the Dog House Bar, where guests can bring their own liquor and are given a small locker in which to keep it. The Dog House has a rough, western saloon atmosphere where riders can cool off after a day on the trails. The card room comes complete with its own legend. It seems that a long time ago, bandits broke in and threatened to hang the owner to force him to disclose the whereabouts of the $85,000 he was supposed to have stashed away. He either faced the bandits down or was strung up, depending on who's telling the tale.

A lot
of bunk.

Unpretentious western ease and comfort characterize accommodations at the ranch. The dining room, above, is filled with sunlight.

In the evening, most of the guests are quite tired, especially the ones who have availed themselves of the unlimited riding. The ranch also offers a number of other activities—usually sedentary ones, such as watching an old movie travelogue or listening to a talk by a forest ranger on the various flora in the area. There are, for example, century plants, used in making an Arizonan version of tequila, and the giant saguaro cacti, which became symbolic of this part of the country to generations of Americans who never came closer to Arizona than a Saturday Hopalong Cassidy matinee. For the more spirited, there are square dances.

The sound of the birds and the voices of the wind in the leaves of the quaking aspens give way to the awesome silence of Grand View, with mountain peaks stretching out for miles above the hushed valley below. Just beyond Road Runner Ridge is a desolate valley where visitors can be completely alone and undisturbed. Just a short distance from each guest room is another world—the magnificent Old West.

147

Midnight luxury.

After a hard day's riding on the range, the aches and cares fall away in the swirling hot waters of Tanque Verde's spa.

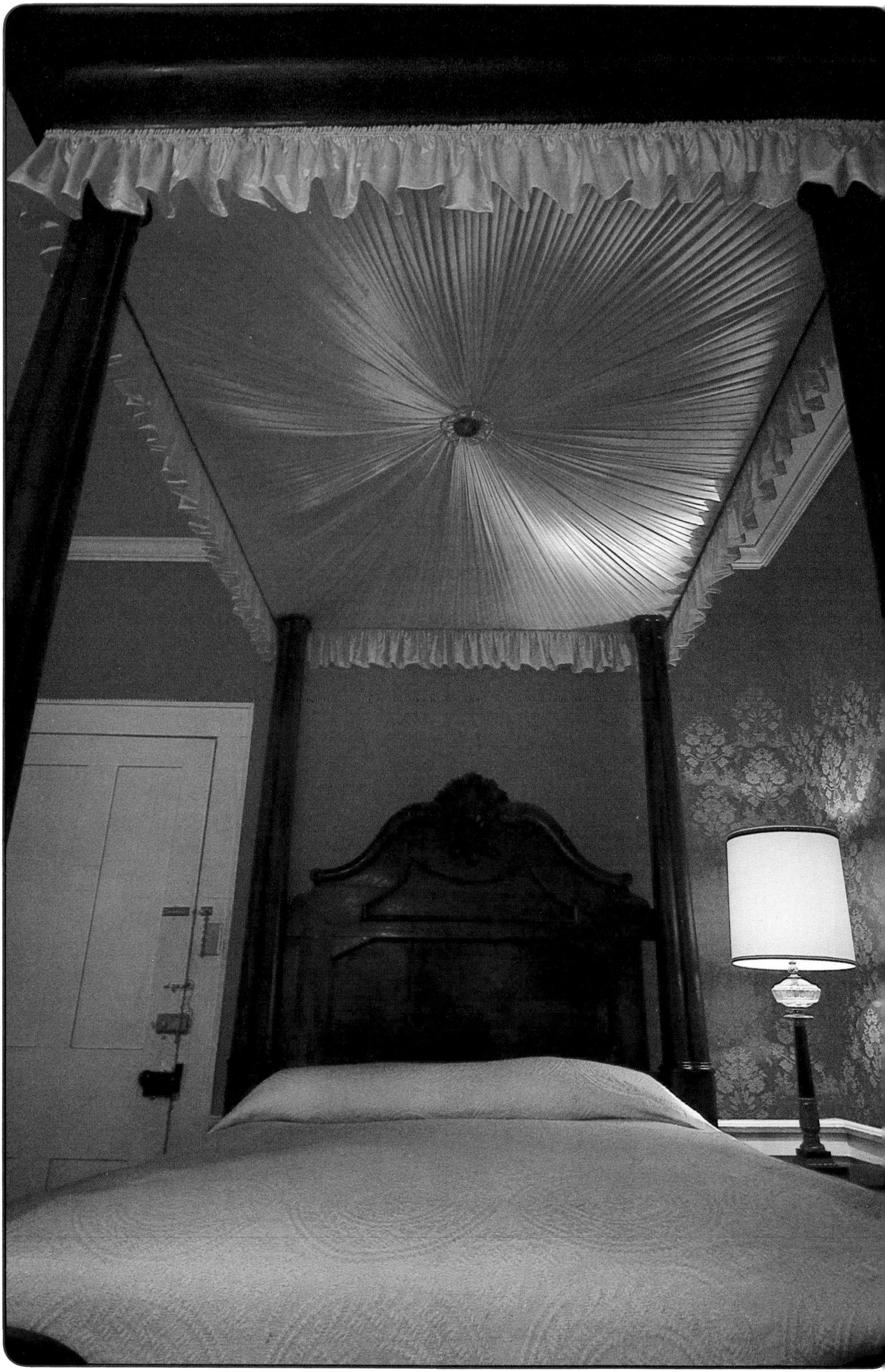

A modest
front

on the town street conceals
the Jefferson's decorative
treasures, while the New
England church, inset,
adds variety to the town's
architecture.

EXCELSIOR HOUSE

Jefferson, Texas

According to one of the men he wiped out in a particularly shoddy piece of stock manipulation, "Jay Gould is the worst man on earth since the beginning of Christendom." This somewhat bleak estimation of the famous nineteenth-century robber baron was by no means a minority opinion. Gould cheerfully admitted he was "the most hated man in America." He probably was not much concerned. Before his death from tuberculosis in 1892, Gould calculated he owned one out of every ten miles of railroad in the country.

One of the few times the old brigand was ever stopped cold was in Jefferson, Texas. In the late 1870s, Jefferson was a booming shipping point for southwestern cotton. Gould came to the town with grandiose plans for turning it into a huge railroad center. When the city fathers were shortsighted enough to demand that Gould actually pay for his line's right of way, the financier became furious. He stormed over to the Excelsior House and in a rage scrawled, "The end of Jefferson!" in the registration book. Gould's prophecy almost came true. When the main rail lines went elsewhere, Jefferson was turned into a virtual ghost town as the population dwindled from 35,000 to less than 3,000. But if it lost its commercial preeminence, it gained a priceless heritage. Although Jefferson did not prosper, at least it was not torn down to make way for a twentieth-century metropolis. Its original structures stayed much as they had been for almost one hundred years.

In the late 1950s, the ladies of the Jesse Allen Wise Garden Club initiated a vigorous campaign to restore Jefferson to its glory days. Their prize restoration is the old Excelsior House. The club members swarmed over the hotel—scraping, sanding, refinishing and reupholstering every piece of furniture in the place. Although mostly amateurs,

Gathered
velvet

tops the magnificent
canopied bed in one room of
the Presidential Suite at the
Excelsior.

The front desk

was covered by three coats of paint, which the ladies restoring the hotel removed before returning it to its original, natural finish. The register has recorded the names of many famous guests through the years.

The parlor

contains "store-bought" furniture where fantasy has run riot. Citations on the wall honor the hotel's restoration.

in 1961 they received a special governor's citation for one of the finest restorations in the state.

In its day, the Excelsior was one of the premier hotels in the Southwest, made of brick and timber, with a lacy, ironwork gallery in the front to give it a touch of Louisiana. In fact, in the nineteenth century, the Excelsior was the site of the Queen Mab balls, which were part of their own Mardi Gras celebration, with parades and floats that rivaled anything in New Orleans at the time. The Excelsior drew famous guests from all over the world. The Barrymores always took a suite here when their touring company came to town. Oscar Wilde was enchanted by the formal patio garden in the back when he stopped here during his whirlwind lecture tour of America in 1882. The hotel was a great favorite with the members of the nineteenth-century American social aristocracy such as the Vanderbilts and the Whitneys. Presidents Ulysses S. Grant and Rutherford B. Hayes both entertained in the lavishly decorated ballroom.

All fourteen upstairs rooms are furnished with delightful museum-

quality country antiques of maple, cherry and mahogany. Lady Bird Johnson went to high school in Jefferson and has taken a special interest in the restoration of the Excelsior and in the rest of the community. The gold clock over the main fireplace is a gift from the former first lady. She visits the Excelsior often and once noted a table that was similar to, but nicer than, the one in the Lincoln Room at the White House made by the eminent Victorian cabinetmaker, John H. Belter.

Cissie McCampbell has been manager of the Excelsior for more than fifteen years and still supervises her famous plantation breakfasts in a sunny nook off the garden in the back. Breakfast at the Excelsior, the only meal served except for special parties, is hearty Texas fare consisting of bacon, eggs, grits, freshly squeezed orange juice and Cissie's own special bite-size Orange Blossom muffins, which literally melt in one's mouth.

An
open
invitation
to nostalgia, the Excelsior's ballroom, left, and dining room, right, feature pieces that show the hotel's importance as a nineteenth-century gathering place. The table in the ballroom is by Belter. The dining room's antique Rococo chandelier is from Dresden.

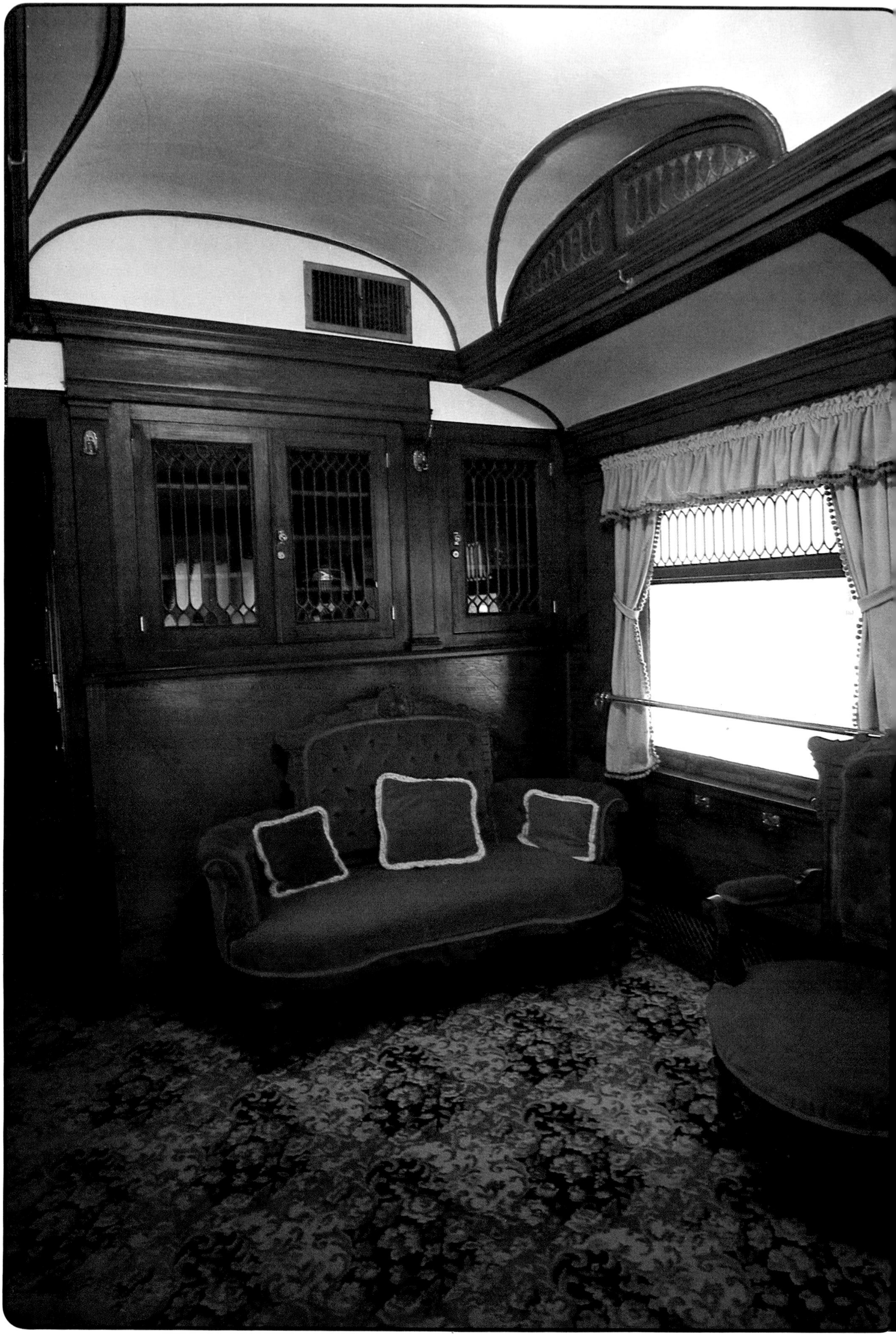

The scoundrel's lair.

Two views of Jay Gould's private railway car, *Atalanta*, restored by the Excelsior House. It sits near the inn and is open to visitors, for whom it recalls the former glory of nineteenth-century railroading.

The town of Jefferson is a delightful place for a quiet stroll and a relaxed historical tour. The Jefferson Museum, a handsome, red brick building, houses more than three thousand items that trace the development of this southwestern river town. The Carnegie Library, a fine old Classical Revival structure, contains one of the finest collections of old dolls in the state.

One ironic sight in Jefferson is right across the street from the Excelsior. This is *Atalanta*, Jay Gould's old private railroad car, which was discovered in a weed patch many years ago. The Garden Club has restored the car completely, and its mahogany and brocades sparkle as they did in the days when Jay Gould insisted on changing into evening clothes every night for dinner, even when dining alone in his private parlor car. The Garden Club charges a fifty-cent admission fee, and the people of Jefferson think it funny that after all these years, they are finally making some money off Jay Gould.

THE INNS

Even an institution as timeless as a country inn is changeable. Ownerships are transferred, rooms are redecorated and chefs come and go. Undoubtedly some changes will be made in the establishments written about here. But their general character and appeal will most likely remain intact. In spite of changes, or perhaps because of them, most of these inns have already stood the test of time. Most changeable of all are rates, of course, but current rates are given so that readers will have a clear idea of the range of expense for each establishment. Reservations are necessary for accommodations at all the inns. Maps are provided only for those inns the editors felt particularly hard to locate. In regard to children and pets, it is best to ask each inn specifically about its policy.

ARIZONA INN, 2200 East Elm Street, Tucson, Arizona 85719; (602) 325-1541, Robert Minerich, Innkeeper. An 86-room inn, located on 14 acres near the University of Arizona campus in suburban Tucson. Open all year. Room rates vary. From May through December, single occupancy is $29 to $43; double, $37 to $48; suites from $60. From January to April, single occupancy is $56 to $82; double, $62 to $88; suites from $95. Private and shared baths. Restaurant serves breakfast, lunch and dinner. American Express, Master Charge, Visa and Carte Blanche credit cards accepted. Heated swimming pool, tennis courts, putting green and badminton.

DIRECTIONS: From I-10, take Speedway Boulevard east to the University of Arizona. Turn left on Campbell; five blocks down, turn right onto East Elm.

BURGUNDY HOUSE, 6711 Washington Street, Yountville, California 94599; (707) 944-2711, Mary and Bob Keenan, Innkeepers. A 12-room inn in a Napa Valley wine country town. Open all year. Double occupancy rates are $45, including Continental breakfast. Some shared baths. No credit cards accepted.

DIRECTIONS: From Cal. 29 take Yountville exit, drive north through town on Washington Street to the inn.

THE CAPTAIN WHIDBEY, Route 1, Box 32, Coupeville, Washington 98329; (206) 678-4097, Steve and Shirlie Stone and sons, Innkeepers. A 25-room inn with restaurant on Whidbey Island. Open all year. Room rates range from $20 to $40, double occupancy, with Continental breakfast during the winter. Private and shared baths. Restaurant serves breakfast, lunch and dinner throughout most of the year; in winter, lunch and dinner only. Master Charge and Visa credit cards accepted. Boating and fishing.

DIRECTIONS: The inn is at Penn Cove 3 miles NW of Coupeville on Whidbey Island. From Seattle drive north to Mukilteo, SW of Everett, and take the ferry to Columbia Beach and then Wash. 525 to Coupeville. From Vancouver-Bellingham take I-5 to Burlington and Wash. 20 west to Whidbey Island and south to Penn Cove. There is also a ferry from Port Townsend to Whidbey Island. Once there, drive north on 20 to Coupeville and Penn Cove.

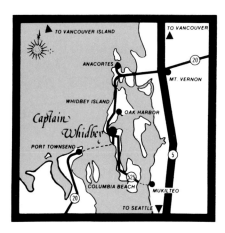

CITY HOTEL, Main Street, Columbia, California 95301; (209) 532-1479, Vicky Shanklin-Bratten, Innkeeper. A 9-room hotel in a re-created Gold Rush town. Open all year. Room rates range from $27.50 to $39.50, double occupancy, including Continental breakfast. Private half-baths, with shower down the hall. Restaurant serves lunch and dinner daily. Master Charge and Visa charge cards accepted.

DIRECTIONS: Located 3 miles north of Sonora on Route 49. The inn is on Main Street, which is closed to traffic during the day. Take the alternate road going around the town center and park in back of the hotel.

EXCELSIOR HOUSE, 211 West Austin Street, Jefferson, Texas 75657; (214) 665-2513, Cissie McCampbell, Innkeeper. Open all year. Double occupancy rates range from $14 to $18; two-bedroom suites available for $30. Private and shared baths. Full breakfast additional. No credit cards accepted.

DIRECTIONS: Jefferson is about 200 miles east of Dallas and 250 miles north of Houston. The inn is located off Polk Street, in the heart of Jefferson.

HERITAGE HOUSE, 5200 Highway 1, Little River, California 95456; (707) 937-5885, L. D. Dennan, Innkeeper. A 50-room inn on the coast of northern California. Open February through November. Rates range from $34 to $73 for single occupancy, from $57 to $87 double occupancy; 2-room suites range from $82 to $97. Each additional person in any accommodation is charged $20. Private baths. Rates include dinner and breakfast. No credit cards accepted.

DIRECTIONS: The inn is on Cal. 1 in Little River, five miles north of the intersection of Routes 128 and 1.

THE INN AT RANCHO SANTA FE, P.O. Box 869, Ranch Santa Fe, California 92067; (714) 756-1131, Dan D. Royce, Innkeeper. A 75-room inn, with accommodations spread out over private cottages. Open all year. Room rates vary from $38 to $150, depending on the accommodation and the number of people. Restaurant serves breakfast, lunch and dinner. Major credit cards accepted.

DIRECTIONS: The inn is located on Paseo Delicias, the main street of Rancho Santa Fe. Take I-5 to exit 58 and drive inland about 5 miles.

JAMES HOUSE, 1238 Washington Street, Port Townsend, Washington 98368; (206) 385-1238, Lowell and Barbara Bogart, Innkeepers. A 10-room Victorian guest house in an old seaport town on the Olympic Peninsula. Open all year. Rates range from $24 for a single, $28 for a double, to $40 for the Bridal Suite. All include Continental breakfast. Private and shared baths. No credit cards accepted.

DIRECTIONS: In Port Townsend, the James House is in the upper town, on the road running along the edge of the bluff, next to the Post Office.

MacCALLUM HOUSE, P.O. Box 206, Mendocino, California 95460; (707) 937-0289, Bill and Sue Norris, Innkeepers. A 24-room inn with restaurant on the northern California coast. Open all year. Room rates range from $34.50 to $45.50, double occupancy, including Continental breakfast. Private and shared baths. Restaurant serves dinner daily from April to December. Master Charge and Visa credit cards accepted.

DIRECTIONS: Mendocino is just off Cal. 1, the coast highway. Turn right at the first major intersection in Mendocino, then first left. The inn is on the right, halfway down the block.

RANCHO ENCANTADO, P.O. Box 570, Santa Fe, New Mexico 87501; (505) 982-3537, Betty Egan, Innkeeper. A 28-room ranch resort in the New Mexico Chaparral country. Open from shortly after Easter to the end of October. Room rates average $65, double occupancy; suites available. Restaurant serves breakfast, lunch and dinner. All major credit cards accepted. Tennis courts, swimming pool, shooting range, horseback riding.

DIRECTIONS: Take I-84 north from Santa Fe to the Tesuque exit. Take N.M. 22 past Tesuque about 2 miles to inn sign on right. The inn is a mile down the road.

ST. ORRES, P.O. Box 523, Gualala, California 95445; (707) 884-3303; Eric Black, Rick Wasserman, Rosemary Campiformio, Ted Black, Innkeepers. An 8-room inn, built by its proprietors, on the coast. Open all year. Room rates range from $35 to $45, double occupancy, including Continental breakfast. Shared baths. Restaurant serves dinner every evening. Master Charge and Visa credit cards accepted.

DIRECTIONS: Located on Cal. 1, 106 miles north of San Francisco, 1 mile north of Gualala.

SALISHAN LODGE, P.O. Box 118, Gleneden Beach, Oregon 97388; (503) 764-2371, Alex Murphy, Innkeeper. A 150-room resort on the coast of northern Oregon. Open all year. Double occupancy rates range from $38 to $52, depending on the season. Private baths. Restaurant serves breakfast, lunch and dinner. American Express, Visa and Master Charge credit cards accepted. Golf course, tennis courts, hiking trails, swimming pool, ocean beach.

DIRECTIONS: Located on Or. 101, midway between Depoe Bay and Lincoln City, near the center of town. Watch for sign.

SAN YSIDRO RANCH, 900 San Ysidro Lane, Montecito, California 93108; (805) 969-5046, Jim and Susie Lavenson, Innkeepers. 39 individual cottages with stable facilities. Open all year. Rates range from $45 to $189, double occupancy. Restaurant serves breakfast, lunch and dinner. Major credit cards accepted. Tennis courts, swimming pool.

DIRECTIONS: Take San Ysidro Road east through Montecito Village to San Ysidro Lane.

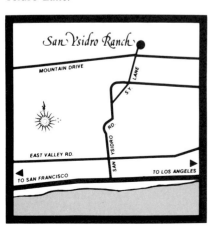

SONOMA HOTEL, 110 West Spain Street, Sonoma, California 95476; (707) 996-2996, John and Dorene Musilli, Innkeepers. A 17-room hotel in a historic town in California's wine country. Open all year. Room rates range from $28 to $45, double occupancy, including Continental breakfast. Shared baths. American Express, Master Charge and Visa credit cards accepted.

DIRECTIONS: Hotel is on the northwest corner of the Sonoma town plaza.

SUTTER CREEK INN, 73 Main Street, Sutter Creek, California 95685; (209) 267-5606, Jane Way, Innkeeper. A 16-room inn at the center of a village in the Gold Rush country. Open all year, except the first two weeks in January. Rates range from $28 to $42, double occupancy, depending on the particular room and whether accommodations are for midweek or weekend. Rate for the Carriage House is $55. Private baths. All rates include full breakfast. No children under 10 years old. No pets. No credit cards accepted.

DIRECTIONS: Located 20 miles east of Sacramento, off Route 49.

TANQUE VERDE RANCH, P.O. Box 66, Tucson, Arizona 85710; (602) 296-6275, Bob and DeeDee Cote, Innkeepers. 60 secluded cottages in the foothills of the Rincon Mountains. Open all year. Room rates vary with the season and the accommodation, and all include horseback riding privileges. From May through November, single occupancy is $50 to $65; double occupancy, $70 to $90. From December through April single occupancy is $70 to $90; double occupancy, $80 to $110. Restaurant serves meals to guests only. No credit cards accepted. Indoor and outdoor pools, tennis, sauna.

DIRECTIONS: Take the Speedway all the way to the end. Inn is on the left.

TIMBERLINE LODGE, Government Camp, Oregon 97028, (503) 272-3311; Richard L. Kohnstamm, Innkeeper. A 50-room ski lodge on the side of Mount Hood, east of Portland. Open all year. Room rates range from $30 to $60, double occupancy. Private baths. Restaurant serves breakfast, lunch and dinner daily. American Express, Master Charge and Visa credit cards accepted. Year-round skiing, swimming pool.

DIRECTIONS: On I-26, watch for signs near Government Camp indicating the road up to the lodge.

UNION HOTEL, 362 Bell Street, Los Alamos, California 93440; (to telephone, dial operator and ask for 2744 in Los Alamos). Richard and Teri Langdon, Innkeepers. A 14-bedroom frontier hotel, faithfully restored to its original condition. Open all year, but on weekends only, from Friday through Sunday. Double occupancy rates range from $30 to $40, with full breakfast. Private and shared baths. Restaurant serves dinner only. No children or pets. No credit cards accepted.

DIRECTIONS: Located in the center of Los Alamos, on the main street.

VAGABOND HOUSE, P.O. Box 2747, Carmel-by-the-Sea, California 93921; (408) 624-9988, Chuck and Patsy Watts, Innkeepers. A 12-room inn in an oceanside resort town. Open all year. Room rates range from $30 to $42, double occupancy, including Continental breakfast. Some rooms have full kitchen. Private baths. No credit cards accepted. No children; no pets.

DIRECTIONS: Take Carmel exits off Cal. 1. Drive down Ocean Avenue, Carmel's main street, to Dolores, turn right. Inn is 2½ blocks up on the right.

WINE COUNTRY INN, 1152 Lodi Lane, St. Helena, California 95474; (707) 963-7077, Ned and Marge Smith and Jim Smith, Innkeepers. A 15-room country inn built in the style of early Napa Valley buildings. Open all year. Room rates range from $40 to $45, double occupancy, including Continental breakfast. Private baths. Master Charge and Visa credit cards accepted.

DIRECTIONS: Cal. 29 through the Napa Valley. North of St. Helena, 2 miles, turn at sign for Lodi Lane. The inn's entrance is just down the road, on the left.

Photograph on page one taken in Sonoma County by Lilo Raymond

Frontispiece photograph taken at the Union Hotel by George W. Gardner

Title page photograph taken at Heritage House by Lilo Raymond

A ROBERT REID, WIESER AND WIESER PRODUCTION CREATED FOR THE KNAPP PRESS, LOS ANGELES
WITH THE EDITORS OF ARCHITECTURAL DIGEST
EDITORIAL ASSOCIATES: GEORGE ALLEN AND TRACY ECCLESINE
DESIGNED AND PRODUCED BY THE VINJE, REID DESIGN STUDIO
COLOR SEPARATIONS BY OFFSET SEPARATIONS CORP, NEW YORK
TYPESET BY THE MONOTYPE COMPOSITION COMPANY, BALTIMORE
PRINTED BY CLARK FRANKLIN KINGSTON PRESS, BOSTON
BOUND BY THE BOOK PRESS, BRATTLEBORO, VERMONT